100

THINGS TO DO IN

ARLINGTON
VIRGINIA

BEFORE YOU

DIE

Arlington National Cemetery

100

THINGS TO DO IN

ARLINGTON VIRGINIA

BEFORE YOU

DIE

• •

BARBARA NOE KENNEDY

Library of Congress Control Number: 2023951762

ISBN: 9781681065137

Design by Jill Halpin

All images are courtesy of the author unless otherwise noted.

Printed in the United States of America
24 25 26 27 28   5 4 3 2 1

We (the publisher and the author) have done our best to provide the most accurate information available when this book was completed. However, we make no warranty, guarantee, or promise about the accuracy, completeness, or currency of the information provided, and we expressly disclaim all warranties, express or implied. Please note that attractions, company names, addresses, websites, and phone numbers are subject to change or closure, and this is outside of our control. We are not responsible for any loss, damage, injury, or inconvenience that may occur due to the use of this book. When exploring new destinations, please do your homework before you go. You are responsible for your own safety and health when using this book.

DEDICATION

To my husband, David Kennedy, who has helped me
make Arlington home.

Lost Dog Cafe

CONTENTS

• •

● ●

Sports and Recreation

● ●

Culture and History

• •

• •

Shopping and Fashion

Covet

PREFACE

I have lived in Arlington for decades and consider myself pretty well versed in what our city offers. I love running and biking its trails, eating at the international mix of local restaurants (though you'll find my husband and me at Lost Dog nearly every Friday— our version of Cheers), showing off the big-name sites to visitors, including Arlington National Cemetery, and I will never tire of that classic view along the Potomac River from the Mount Vernon Trail, peering at the nation's most iconic monuments reflected in the shimmering river waters.

But as I embarked on researching this book, peeling back the layers and digging beneath the surface, I was surprised at—and excited to discover—what I didn't know. George Washington owned a forest here. John Ball's extant 18th-century house, hidden in a residential neighborhood, provides a glimpse at how ordinary people lived (i.e., not George Washington at his famous Mount Vernon). This is truly an artsy town, with its public art program recently celebrating its 40th anniversary—and more than 80 public works of art sprinkled throughout the city. I had no clue about the story behind Weenie Beenie. There's even a tucked-away outdoor restaurant that exudes a vacay feel with froufrou drinks and plein air eating overlooking a boat-filled marina.

My research also uncovered stories embarrassingly unknown to me, including how African American communities were destroyed in the name of progress. I knew about Freedman's Village, within Arlington National Cemetery (there's only a historical plaque left), but I had no idea that the residents of

Queen City were callously displaced when the Pentagon was built during World War II. Surprisingly, I learned about that at an art sprinkled park built by a new neighbor in town—Amazon, whose new headquarters I visited (admittedly) with some trepidation. I knew the innocuous-looking wall virtually in my own backyard was called segregation wall, but I didn't know the specifics about how it separated an all-White neighborhood from an all-Black neighborhood, and that the little park I drive by nearly every day on Langston Boulevard honors the formerly enslaved individuals who lived there and their descendants. I have to say, I'm proud of how Arlington has made these important stories accessible rather than burying them.

In the end, after traipsing all over a city I thought I knew, I gleaned a whole new understanding of Arlington (and I know that Arlington officially is a county and not a city, but I've referred to it as a city throughout this book because to me, county doesn't encapsulate its vibrancy). We have a fabulous city here, with lots of things to do that really do add joy, understanding, and fun, and that offer a richer life. This book is not meant to be a comprehensive list, but to provide impetus to pique your curiosity about Arlington's many glorious facets. So, go out and explore our amazing city! In addition to these suggestions, you'll discover even more places and come up with your own list of places that will touch you one way or another.

Happy rambling.

—Barbara Noe Kennedy

Note: Pentagon City and Crystal City may be rebranded as National Landing, as part of Amazon's H2Q headquarters. As of press time, the final rebranding is still in flux. Therefore, I've stuck with the original terms for these neighborhoods because they remain the names of the Metro stops.

• •

Lost Dog Cafe

FOOD
AND DRINK

GIVE SOME DOGGY LOVE
AT LOST DOG CAFE

Creative gourmet sandwiches and pizzas—and a masterfully culled selection of beers on tap and hundreds more in bottles and cans—are the mainstays of this longtime favorite eatery in Westover Village. And while it's a nice place to come for a Mighty Dog or Buffalo Beagle sandwich, there's more. Hint: it has something to do with all the paintings of dogs that smother the walls. You see, Lost Dog is all about rescuing humans' best friends. The Lost Dog & Cat Rescue Foundation, established in 2001, has found more than 45,000 forever homes through rescue and adoption. What's not to like about that?

Today, there are five Lost Dog restaurants in the region—each one owned by former employees and members of the Lost Dog Cafe family.

5876 Washington Blvd., Westover Village, 703-237-1552
lostdogcafe.com

TIP

Lost Dog's associate restaurant, Stray Cat Bar & Grill, just a few shops down from the Westover location, has a cat theme; its menu focuses more on burgers and salads (and its paintings depict cats). It tends to be quieter than Lost Dog.

5866 Washington Blvd., 703-237-7775
straycatgrill.com

BE TEMPTED
AT HEIDELBERG PASTRY SHOPPE

Try to walk into this popular German/European bakery on Langston Boulevard without being tantalized by delectable Danish, scones, cookies, and fresh bread—many made with authentic German flour. You can't. They also have German-style deli sandwiches, sausages served on homemade buns, and bauernwurst, a pork-and-beef sausage studded with mustard seeds.

No doubt Heidelberg shines the most during the holidays. Christmas showcases Heidelberg's stollen, a fruit bread made with nuts, spices, and/or candied fruit. New Year's features adorable marzipan pigs with coins in their mouths, while Easter highlights hot cross buns. Halloween, presidential elections, and the Super Bowl all bring fancifully decorated sugar cookies. And here's an interesting tidbit: they've also won their fair share of awards for their wedding cakes.

Pastry chef and baker Wolfgang Büchler opened the shop in 1975—naming it after his hometown—and he still runs the show with his wife, Arlington native Carla.

2150 N Culpeper St. at Langston Blvd., 703-527-8394
heidelbergbakery.com

FREQUENT ONE LAST
LITTLE SAIGON HOLDOUT AT NAM-VIET

After the fall of Saigon in 1975, the Clarendon neighborhood attracted many Vietnamese refugees, establishing what was called Little Saigon. Vietnamese groceries, shops, and restaurants filled the area, with annual festivals and flea markets buzzing with activity. Sadly, the Vietnamese family businesses eventually declined as sparkling high-rises, residential buildings, and modern chain shops took their places.

Since that time, the only remaining business is Nam-Viet (aka Pho 79), opened in 1986 and still run by the Nguyen family. When you find it, you're in for a treat. Yes, they serve pho and bun, which are quite good, but on their packed menu, you'll also discover hard-to-find Vietnamese fare such as crispy glazed baby back ribs, caramelized catfish in a clay pot, and wild salmon with jalapeños, ginger, and onions. An unassuming bar in back creates frilly umbrella drinks. Be sure to check out the wall of photographs, which includes former American POWs, politicos, and presidents who have all dined here.

Note: a five-stop walking tour through Clarendon yields a quick history of Little Saigon; look for five stickers with QR codes on former Vietnamese businesses that showcase archival photos and oral histories on littlesaigonclarendon.com.

1127 N Hudson St., Clarendon, 703-522-7110
namvietva.com

HERE ARE THREE MORE FANTASTIC VIETNAMESE RESTAURANTS IN TOWN

Chill Zone
Delicious pho in a cool café setting, but also keto dishes, creative frappés, and delicious coffee.
2442 N Harrison St., 703-270-9466
chillzonecafe.com

Four Sisters Grill
An outpost of the Lai family's now-defunct Four Sisters restaurant, featuring their famous pho, spring rolls, and papaya salad.
3035 Clarendon Blvd., 703-243-9020
foursistersgrill.com

Pho 75
Established in 1985 and still going strong, serving what many claim to be the region's best pho.
1721 Wilson Blvd., 703-525-7355
facebook.com/profile.php?id=100069161901236

GET TO KNOW
RUTHIE'S ALL-DAY

It's not one of Arlington's old-timers, yet, and it's in the oddest location, off a residential part of Glebe Road amid apartment buildings. But in the time that Ruthie's All-Day has been around (since September 2020), it has changed our dining-scape. The chef, Matt Hill, is a James Beard finalist, after all. The menu has a southern bent, given Hill's North Carolina roots (Ruthie was his grandmother). There's a custom wood smoker that flavors much of the menu—beef brisket, pork spare ribs, and half-rack sticky spare ribs—though there is plenty of other fare too, including salmon, shrimp, and more. All are served with "two" or "three" sides (the mac and cheese is to die for!). Creative salads, sandwiches, and a stellar cocktail program are all inviting as well. The expansive patio is the place to be on warm summer nights.

Do not admit to anyone you've dined here without ordering the sweet skillet cornbread with a side of honey butter or the fryer hush puppies filled with minced shrimp and jalapeño. THAT alone will change your life. Yum!

3411 5th St. S, 703-888-2841
ruthiesallday.com

CHEF MATT HILL CAME FROM THE LIBERTY TAVERN RESTAURANT GROUP, WHICH OVERSEES THREE MORE ARLINGTON FAVORITES, ALL IN CLARENDON.

The Liberty Tavern
A popular neighborhood bar serving elevated pub fare.
3195 Wilson Blvd., 703-465-9360
thelibertytavern.com

Lyon Hall
A European brasserie with delicious mussel pots.
3100 N Washington Blvd., 703-741-7636
lyonhallarlington.com

Northside Social
A modern coffee shop and gathering place in a historic house.
3211 Wilson Blvd., 703-465-0145
northsidesocialva.com

EAT HEALTHY BUT YUMMY
AT SILVER DINER

It may look retro, but decades-old Silver Diner in Ballston is all about farm-sourced, flexitarian, healthy meals prepared with seasonal flair. Whether it's salmon, Thanksgiving turkey platter, braised brisket, or fried chicken (okay, maybe not all are so healthy) on its enormous, catch-all menu, you can bet it's fresh, delicious, and local. Breakfast is served all day (apple-pie-stuffed French toast, anyone?) and tropical mimosas are a favorite. It's also a popular, late-night destination for the after-hours crowd.

The cofounder and executive chef is the amazing Ype Von Hengst. He even won the $10,000 prize on *Chopped* and donated his winnings to Doctors without Borders.

4400 Wilson Blvd., Ballston, 703-812-8600
silverdiner.com/ballston

TIP
There are more than 20 Silver Diner locations across the region (including one of the latest, a rooftop dining lounge overlooking Nationals Park in Washington, DC). The original Silver Diner was founded in 1989 in Rockville, Maryland.

GET A TASTE OF NAPOLI
AT A MODO MIO

While A Modo Mio is relatively new (established in 2020) and hasn't paid the dues to become a firmly established Arlington entity, it's clear it has all the potential to do so. Biting into the Margherita pizza (half-price during happy hour!), you will feel instantly transported to Pizzeria Brandi in Naples, where, according to popular tradition, this mouthwatering concoction of mozzarella cheese, basil, and tomatoes (the colors of the Italian flag, named for Italy's Queen Margherita) was invented in 1889. This is seriously good food, using only Italian flour and baked in an official Napoli oven.

And if you don't want to take our word for it, take the word of 50 Top Pizza, a pizza evaluation site in Italy that in 2023 ranked A Modo Mio as one of the top 50 pizza places in the entire United States—they ranked 48th. Pretty good for a new kid on the block.

5555 Langston Blvd., 703-532-0990
amodomiopizza.com

FOLLOW THE STARS
TO EL POLLO RICO

For Arlingtonians who love their Peruvian barbecue chicken, the one chicken joint that wins hands down is the legendary El Pollo Rico. Victor Solano established this tiny, plain restaurant in 1988 to share a bit of his native Peru with Arlington. But it's anything but lackluster. Visitors who have made their way here include tennis powerhouse Serena Williams and late foodie icon Anthony Bourdain—you know they don't frequent just any restaurant, especially one that has counter-only service. Bourdain said the success comes in the marinade.

Whatever the case, the charbroiled chicken with crispy skin, spiced to perfection with cumin, garlic, and citrus, is succulent and delicious. Each meal comes with two house-made sauces (yellow and spicy green—ask for extra) and your choice of two sides—crispy fries, creamy coleslaw, plantains, fried yucca, or rice and beans (opt for the fries). Order an Inca cola to go with, and you're set.

There are also locations in Woodbridge, Fairfax, and Wheaton, Maryland.

932 N Kenmore St., Virginia Square, 703-522-3220
elpollorico.com

HERE ARE TWO OTHER PERUVIAN CHICKEN PLACES IN TOWN THAT HAVE ALSO WON ACCOLADES

Crisp & Juicy
Delicious but a little on the pricey side.
4540 Cherry Hill Rd., 703-243-4222
crispjuicy.com

Super Pollo Charcoal Chicken
Popular Peruvian chicken but also fried fish and subs.
5011 Wilson Blvd., 703-351-7666
ordersuperpollocharcoalchicken.com

CRACK CRABS
AT QUARTERDECK

If you are craving Maryland cracked crab, don't drive all the way to the Chesapeake. Quarterdeck, tucked away in the Fort Myers Heights neighborhood since 1979, has the same bay vibe (well, without the bay) on its enormous outdoor patio, offering a feast of steamed blue crabs doused in Old Bay seasoning. You can order the crustaceans by the half dozen or dozen—or all you can eat—and pound away to your heart's content on the newspaper-covered tables; mallets are provided. Complements include corn on the cob, hush puppies, and pitchers of ice-cold beer. Landlubbers can enjoy steak, chicken, and pizza (but why?!). Top it all off with a slice of pie: Key lime, red velvet, or the odd-yet-yummy blueberry cream.

1200 Fort Myer Dr., Fort Myers Heights, 703-528-2722
quarterdeckarlington.com

EAT AMAZING DRUNKEN NOODLES
AT THAI NOY

Thai restaurants come and go, but Thai Noy has been a neighborhood mainstay for decades. Kot Symoukda founded the restaurant in 2001; unfortunately, he passed away in 2019, but the family continues to prepare the homestyle drunken noodles, basil chicken, and tom yum goong (hot-and-sour shrimp soup) that everyone loves, using old family recipes. There are unexpected items too, including pine-nut chicken, grilled salmon in red curry and coconut sauce, and dancing squid (stir-fried squid in peppers, basil, and onions). You can take out, but the cozy restaurant, with orchids and Thai art on the walls depicting the Ramayana and gilded Buddhas, is inviting. You can also dine on the red-painted deck overlooking the parking lot.

5880 Washington Blvd., Westover Village, 703-534-7474
thainoy.com

ENJOY
A LIFE OF PIE

One of life's greatest gifts is pie—and Arlingtonians are blessed with not one but two amazing pie shops, serving up the flakiest, fruitiest, most delicious pies around.

Acme Pie Co. on Columbia Pike uses local ingredients in its handmade pies, "just like grandma used to make, if grandma was a pastry chef and made really great pie," they say. These pies will remind you of warm fuzzy blankets, spring rains, and cuddling with your kitty (or dog). Some of the faves: Key lime pie (especially if you love sour), walnut chocolate, and blackberry peach.

The other must-do pie place is Livin' the Pie Life on Glebe, near Langston Boulevard, whose slogan is "born and baked in Arlington." They sell both savory and sweet pastries, so not only can you indulge in strawberry rhubarb, apple caramel crumb, and mile-high (Oreo crust, Valrhona mousse, whipped cream, oh my!) desserts, you may also choose chicken pot pie, quiche, and other assorted goods.

Acme Pie Co.
2803 Columbia Pike, 703-647-9548
acmepieco.com

Livin' the Pie Life
2166 N Glebe Rd., 571-431-7727
livinthepielife.com

TASTE ARLINGTON'S BEST ICE CREAM
AT TOBY'S

Where do you go if you don't feel like having the fancy, over-the-top (and expensive) ice cream that seems to be everywhere these days? Toby's Homemade Ice Cream, of course. This mom-and-pop shop in Westover offers small-batch, homemade ice cream (and milkshakes!) with unique rotating flavors, including real vanilla bean, black raspberry chip, Philippine mango, and espresso chip. Look for seasonal specials, too, such as peach in summer and peppermint stick in winter.

They made a splash in 2021 during the Brood X invasion with their "cicada sundaes" (scoops of chocolate, bittersweet chocolate, and coffee ice cream, chocolate sprinkles, red M&Ms for eyes, and waffle cones for wings). People drove from all over to try them. The special was discontinued after the last cicada burrowed into the ground, and we may have to wait until 2038 for the next batch. In the meantime, keep on the lookout for other creative ice cream dishes.

Oh, and the locally roasted coffee is as good as the ice cream.

There are two other satellite shops: in Vienna and at the new Amazon headquarters at National Landing.

5849-A Washington Blvd., Westover Village, 703-536-7000
tobysicecream.com

TAKE A CULINARY TOUR
AROUND THE WORLD
WITHOUT LEAVING HOME

An around-the-world jet trip is hands-down a once-in-a-lifetime experience. But then, why spend all that money and deal with jet lag when you can explore the world on a single Arlington street? That's right—the Columbia Pike corridor is often referred to as "the world in a zip code." Along the length of the street, you conceivably could hear more than 100 languages, and, given that food is one of the best ways to experience different cultures, it's also home to numerous small, locally owned restaurants owned and run by people from India, Japan, Ethiopia, Thailand, and more. So, leave your passport at home and embark on a whirlwind tour of culinary experiences around the world.

HERE ARE SOME HIGHLIGHTS

Boru Ramen (Japanese)
2915 Columbia Pike, 703-521-2811
boru-ramen.com

The Celtic House Irish Pub & Restaurant (Irish)
2500 Columbia Pike, 703-746-9644
celtichouse.net

City Kabob & Curry House (Indian and Pakistani)
3007 Columbia Pike, 571-257-8816
citykabobhouse.com

Dama Pastry Restaurant & Cafe (Ethiopian)
1505 Columbia Pike, 703-920-5620
damarestaurant.com

El Pike Bolivian Restobar (Bolivian)
4111 Columbia Pike, 703-521-3010
elpikerestaurant.com

Pupatella (Neapolitan Italian)
1621 S Walter Reed Dr., 703-647-9076
pupatella.com

Rincome Thai Cuisine (Thai)
3030 Columbia Pike, 703-979-0144
rincomethai.com

Sofia's Pupusería (El Salvadorean, Honduran, and Peruvian)
3610 Columbia Pike, 571-483-0487
sofiapupuseria.com

HAVE BREAKFAST ALL DAY—AND NIGHT—
AT BOB & EDITH'S DINER

If you're craving hotcakes or country fried steak in the middle of the night, you should have only one thought: Bob & Edith's Diner. Bob and Edith Bolton established this all-day breakfast joint on Columbia Pike in 1969, offering country hams, scrapple, bologna, and a few other simply Southern dishes—plus endless coffee refills. The menu's grown, with extensive lunch and dinner offerings, plus freshly baked pies and hand-spun milkshakes. But the decor remains pretty much the same: Bolton family photos and Dallas Cowboys paraphernalia. Just remember, if you want fancy, go elsewhere. If you want a good old-fashioned breakfast with a side of grease, Bob & Edith's is calling your name.

Five other regional locations include Crystal City and Langston Boulevard.

2310 Columbia Pike, 703-920-6103
bobandedithsdiner.com

BUY A SLICE
AT THE ITALIAN STORE

Walk into this garlic-and-pepper-infused shop in Lyon Village Shopping Center and you'll swear you just stepped into Italy. It's as close as you'll get in Arlington, anyway, thanks to the Tramonte family. With family roots winding back to Calabria and Civitavecchia, Vincent Tramonte founded the Italian Store in 1980 (with Mama Tramonte working her magic in the kitchen from family recipes). He was born in New York City and came to Northern Virginia to practice law, but changed his game plan when he realized the region was lacking in fresh mozzarella and classic Italian subs.

Today, everyone still raves about the subs (especially the Milano, served with two Italian hams, provolone cheese, and Genoa salami), but the New York–style pizza is just as amazing— try Bianca or Nino's. You'll also find many hard-to-find Italian items, including meats, cheeses, chocolates, and cookies imported directly from the mother country, while the wine selection contains hundreds of bottles straight from Italy. There are frozen pastas and pasta sauce (great to stock up on), fresh-made cannoli, or just stop by for coffee—they use the Illy brand.

There's also a location in Westover, with outdoor seating.

3123 Langston Blvd. in Lyon Village Shopping Center, 703-528-6266
italianstore.com

EAT HYPERLOCAL GREENS, DELIVERED RIGHT TO YOUR DOOR,
FROM AREA 2

Area 2 Farms in Shirlington is a flourishing, state-of-the-art indoor farm created in a repurposed paper company and warehouse building. And just like that, it's serving as a model for other similar projects in the area to solve two issues: utilizing all the city's office space that's been empty since the pandemic *and* providing Arlingtonians with produce that doesn't get more local than this.

You definitely want to be a part of this trend! All you have to do is join the farm's community-supported agriculture to get super-fresh greens delivered to your door. You can also take a free tour to see how the plants are grown on a rotating hydroponic system (i.e., all water, no soil, and lots of LED lighting).

2600 S Oxford St., Shirlington Village, 202-507-9282
area2farms.com

TIP

Area 2 isn't the only urban farm in town. You can also find fresh greens—and edible flowers—at Fresh Impact Farms.
5165 Langston Blvd., 202-507-9252 or 571-310-5979
freshimpactfarms.com

GET AN ORIGINAL
HALF SMOKE ALL THE WAY
AT WEENIE BEENIE

It may look like just a retro food shack in need of a touch-up, but Weenie Beenie in Shirlington is the go-to place for an original half smoke, all the way. A "half smoke" is the local sausage bisected horizontally and grilled to a snap; "all the way" adds chili, mustard, relish, and onion. The yellowed, peeling menu also showcases North Carolina–style, vinegar-based barbecue, beef hot dogs, yummy onion rings, and breakfast served all day.

It all started in the early '50s as a roadside hot dog stand serving everyday working people. But Weenie Beenie's gravitas came in 1960, when professional pool hustler Bill Staton won $27,000 on an Arkansas gambling trip, bought the stand, and gave it its name. At one point, there were six Weenie Beenies around town, but the flagship is all that remains.

2680 Shirlington Rd., Shirlington, 703-671-6661
weeniebeenie.net

FUN FACT

The shack lent its name to a Foo Fighters song from the group's first album. Band leader Dave Grohl grew up in the area.

FIND A NON-TRENDY BUT SPECTACULAR BOTTLE OF WINE
AT ARROWINE & CHEESE

Arrowine & Cheese does not follow trends. You won't find what everyone else is drinking or eating at this little wine and cheese shop in the Lee Heights shopping center. Instead, you'll discover unexpected wines and artisanal cheeses that are the happy results of the staff traveling the world and seeking out the best-of-the-best products. That's why people make pilgrimages here from as far as southern Virginia and West Virginia, to see what's new and to stock up.

There's also a deli case filled with charcuterie and a cheese counter that might have as many as 375 different types of cheeses. A handpicked selection of gourmet groceries and a selection of craft beers round out the offerings. If you can't find it here, they'll order it for you. And since they're not just trying to sell their products but to educate their customers, they hold "education tastings" on Fridays and Saturdays (with special tasting discounts). What's not to like?

Lee Heights Shops, 4508 Cherry Hill Rd., Lee Heights, 703-525-0990
arrowine.com

HAVE A DRINK WITH A VIEW
AT SKYDOME

The Instagram-able cocktails may be expensive, but the views are priceless at Skydome, the 360-degree rotating rooftop restaurant perched 15 stories atop the Doubletree by Hilton in Crystal City. As you sip smoky, color-changing concoctions—one sprinkled with 24-karat gold flakes, another stirred with honey from the rooftop apiary—some of the world's most famous glowing marble monuments pass by at your feet, including the Washington Monument, Jefferson Memorial, and Lincoln Memorial, all snuggled alongside the Potomac River.

Dinner is also an option; the eclectic American menu offers mostly tapas selections such as green-curry hummus, truffle mushroom pizza, and grilled octopus, along with a few mains including the Wagyu Burger, Grilled Tomahawk Porkchop, and Sautéed Gnocchi alla Vodka with jumbo shrimp and asparagus.

But honestly, it's the view you'll brag about most.

300 Army Navy Dr., Crystal City, 703-416-4100
hilton.com/en/hotels/dcaaedt-doubletree-washington-dc-crystal-city/dining

SAVOR THE TANTALIZING AROMA OF FRESHLY BAKED BREAD
AT BEST BUNS

The name Best Buns does not sum up the virtues of this divine Shirlington hot spot—though the pecan buns are memorable. The menu, in addition to the heavenly buns, has a spectacular, too-tempting list of artisan breads, including apple monkey bread (!), bagels, rolls, muffins, croissants, cookies, and cupcakes. They also make delicious sandwiches (both breakfast and lunch), salads, soups, and Black Angus burgers. There are even dog biscuits, for four-legged friends to enjoy on the patio alongside their humans (inside seating is limited). Chill out there, then take some home; the menu offers the "doughs and don'ts" of storing and freezing.

There's also a shop in Vienna.

4010 Campbell Ave., Shirlington Village, 703-578-1500
bestbunsbreadco.com

CELEBRATE A SPECIAL OCCASION
AT SFOGLINA

Sfoglina isn't just a pasta house, though its mainstay is handmade classic and seasonal pastas. This is Michelin-starred Chef Fabio Trabocchi's take on Italian comfort food (meaning, more "casual" than his Fiola and Fiola Mare, both in DC), and every visit is an experience. Fabio's inspiration was his father's wooden pasta table, and that's the centerpiece of this Rosslyn eatery—where doughs are rolled and pastas are shaped. Amid a mod-vintage interior featuring hand-blown chandeliers and custom-made tables, you can indulge in ricotta tortellini with almonds and lemon zest; sepia noodles with crab and clams (a seasonal delight); or goat-cheese-filled ravioli San Leo, spiced with lemon and herbs. Or, if you can't decide, order any three of the dozen or so choices for the table, to be shared family style.

But there's more than pasta. There are also small plates such as Nonna Palmina's meatballs, creative salads, a mozzarella bar, and a few meat and seafood entrées. This will be one unforgettable meal, guaranteed.

There are several other Sfoglinas in DC, as well as at Dulles and DCA.

1100 Wilson Blvd., Rosslyn, 703-893-8000
sfoglinapasta.com/rosslyn

TASTE FOR YOURSELF
ARLINGTON'S BEST KABOBS

Arlington Kabob may look like a hole in the wall, but this woman-owned Afghani eatery on Langston Boulevard has served up some of the juiciest, most delicious kabobs around since opening in 2013. The food is cooked twice a day for lunch and dinner, ensuring everything is freshly prepared. The chargrilled chicken kabobs, served with your choice of vegetables and two types of rice, is probably the most popular dish, but there are all kinds of other options, including lamb chops, beef kofta, chicken shawarma wraps, and even tilapia and salmon kabobs! All are served with a side of steaming hot naan, fresh from the tandoor. And remember, all good meals at Arlington Kabob end with the baklava.

5046 Langston Blvd., 703-531-1498
arlingtonkabobva.com

DRINK VIRGINIA WINE

Virginia has established quite a reputation for its wine, but you don't need to spend all day driving to the countryside to sample it (as nice as that is). Arlington has several venues where you can order a flight or glass and do your own wine sampling—both local vino and beyond. Here are some fun places:

Arrowine & Cheese is an amazingly well-stocked wine shop that offers wine tasting on weekends—no charge, and you have experts telling you about each vintage.

Screwtop Wine Bar in Clarendon has more than 40 wines by the glass plus featured monthly flights.

Verre in the Court House neighborhood has a good-value flight program.

WHINO in Ballston Quarter is a restaurant with an art gallery and an impressive wine list. It also has drinking events such as Island Wines Wine Tasting and Tour of Italy.

Arrowine & Cheese
4508 Cherry Hill Rd.
in Lee Heights Shops
703-525-0990
arrowine.com

Screwtop Wine Bar
1025 N Fillmore St.
703-888-0845
screwtopwinebar.com

Verre
2415 Wilson Blvd.
703-253-3878
verrewinebar.com

WHINO
4238 Wilson Blvd., 2nd floor
571-290-3958
whinova.com

HANG OUT
AT NORTHSIDE SOCIAL

First it was Murky Coffee, then in 2010 it became Northside Social Coffee and Wine, but whatever its name, this spot at the top of Clarendon has long been a community gathering place. Occupying a renovated 18th-century house, Northside Social is cozy and welcoming, with a dog-friendly patio out front and a wine bar upstairs. The coffee is roasted and ground on the spot, served up in a dozen or so options from straight-out espresso to honey-vanilla latte. You also can order a pastry or cookie to go with, or, if you're really hungry, a sandwich or salad.

All that said, it's the community vibe that makes Northside special; a full schedule of events includes Monday Trivia and Tuesday Bingo, along with art shows, pop-up markets, paint and sips, and holiday sing-alongs.

A second location is in Falls Church.

3211 Wilson Blvd. near Clarendon, 703-465-0145
northsidesocialva.com

TIP
Rumor has it, Northside is a popular first date venue.

BECAUSE EVERYONE NEEDS CAFFEINE, HERE ARE SOME OTHER FAVORITE COFFEE SHOPS

Bayou Bakery
An offbeat, New Orleans–flavored coffee bar in Court House—be sure to order a beignet.
1515 N Courthouse Rd., 703-243-2410
bayoubakeryva.com

Chill Zone
An intimate, modern, family-run Vietnamese café near Harrison-Lee Shopping Center.
2442 N Harrison St., 703-270-9466
chillzonecafe.com

Commonwealth Joe Coffee Roasters
Interesting drinks include Commonwealth Joe's nitro (cold and steeped coffee that resembles a glass of Guinness), oat milk lattes, and kombucha.
520 12th St. S, Pentagon City, 855-273-9563
commonwealthjoe.com

Village Sweet
Coffee and pastries baked daily from scratch in Westover Village.
5872 Washington Blvd., 703-237-2700
villagesweetbakery.com

BUY FRESH
AT THE ARLINGTON FARMERS MARKET

Looking for the season's juiciest tomato or sweetest ear of corn? Arlington's farmers markets are the places to go, and we are blessed with nine of them. The Arlington Farmers Market at Courthouse was established in 1979, making it one of the area's oldest markets. That's a long time of enjoying fresh parsley, peaches, and pastries! More than 30 farmers and producers crowd into the Courthouse parking lot every Saturday, selling everything from flaky apple pies and fresh turkeys to funny-looking (but delicious) kohlrabi. Unlike most, it's open year-round.

There are also markets at Ballston (Thursdays), Cherrydale (Saturdays), Columbia Pike (Sundays), EatLoco Saturday Market at Met Park, Fairlington (Sundays), Lubber Run (Saturdays), Rosslyn (Wednesdays), and Westover (Sundays). Visit arlingtonva.us/government/topics/urban-agriculture/farmers-markets for more information.

1400 N Courthouse Rd., Courthouse, 703-391-7353
freshfarm.org/markets/arlington

TIP
Most purveyors work the circuit of farmers markets and sell at multiple locations. So, if you can't make it to your favorite wild mushroom stand on Wednesday, it's possible the sellers will be at another market the next day. You can also preorder for pickup.

HELP THE FOOD INSECURE
AT A LITTLE FOOD PANTRY

Arlington is one of the richest counties in the US, but it's important to remember that poverty exists here too. Some individuals and families find it hard to put food on their tables. Arlington is also an exceedingly generous city and there are programs, including the Arlington Food Assistance Center (AFAC), that coordinate volunteer opportunities to help feed those who might be facing food challenges.

Especially heart-warming are the several Little Food Pantries—like Little Free Libraries, but for food—where you can drop off nonperishable food donations to help those in need. If you join the Facebook group Arlington Neighbors Helping Each Other, you can often find updates on the latest needs.

Campbell Elementary
737 S Carlin Springs Rd.

Little Yellow Free Pantry
203 S Fillmore St.

Saint George's Episcopal Church
915 N Oakland St.

TIP
Contact the Arlington Food Assistance Center for more information on how to help those who are food insecure.
2708 S Nelson St., Ballston, 703-845-8486
afac.org

The View of DC

MUSIC
AND ENTERTAINMENT

RELISH THE BEST OF OFF-BROADWAY
AT SIGNATURE THEATRE

You don't need to trudge all the way to New York City (or Washington, DC, for that matter) to enjoy an exceptional show. Signature Theatre in Shirlington has produced award-winning shows—correction: Tony Award–winning, groundbreaking, world-premiere musicals and plays—since 1991, and it's still going strong. It started off in Gunston Middle School's auditorium, then became a black box theater in a converted former auto garage on South Four Mile Run Drive. Along the way, it garnered a reputation for producing daring "signature" productions in a traditionally large-venue world. These days, Signature's current, dramatic, super-modern, $16-million building is a more fitting space for this adventurous enterprise.

One of its secrets to success is celebrating playwrights— notably, Stephen Sondheim, the amazing composer and lyricist known for so many knockouts: *West Side Story*, *Gypsy*, *A Funny Thing Happened on the Way to the Forum*, *Sunday in the Park with George*, and more. Other secrets involve giving life to forgotten works as well as celebrating fresh new projects. The eight-show annual season is eclectic and always grand.

4200 Campbell Ave., Shirlington Village, 703-820-9771
sigtheatre.org

FEEL THE BEAT
AT THE IWO JIMA MEMORIAL

The Iwo Jima Memorial statue is iconic: six Marines planting the US flag on the Japanese island of Iwo Jima after one of World War II's hardest-fought battles. More formally called the US Marine Corps War Memorial, it's based on a Pulitzer Prize–winning photograph by Joe Rosenthal, who captured the moment back in 1945. The sculpture, by Felix W. de Weldon, honors all marines who have fought in defense of the US since 1775, and the American flag flies at full mast 24/7 by presidential decree. On its base you'll find the location and dates of every battle involving the US Marine Corps up to the present time.

It's a beautiful thing to view, this majestic sculpture rising on a knoll outside the Arlington National Cemetery, overlooking the National Mall (with new restrooms nearby!). But it truly comes to life in summer when the US Marine Drum and Bugle Corps parades at sunset on Tuesday evenings, offering a musical extravaganza with lots of pomp and circumstance. It's free and everyone's invited—bring blankets and a picnic. The music is all-American, and you'll find yourself humming all the way home.

US Marine Memorial Cir., 703-289-2500
nps.gov/gwmp/planyourvisit/usmc_memorial.htm

WATCH
THE NATION'S BEST
FOURTH OF JULY FIREWORKS

Arlington has the distinct advantage of not being *in* Washington, DC, but a little distance away, on hilly terrain—making it the perfect spot to watch the nation's fireworks exploding on the National Mall. Hands down, the best place to watch this birthday gift to the nation is from the sprawling lawn in front of the Netherlands Carillon, overlooking one of America's classic panoramas: the marble-glowing Lincoln Memorial, Washington Monument, and US Capitol, all lined up in a row. Everyone spreads out their blankets on the lawn and eats barbecue chicken and potato salad as the sun sets and the anticipation rises. As soon as the fireworks start, tune into PBS's *A Capitol Fourth* show to match the fireworks to music—culminating in Tchaikovsky's thrilling *1812 Overture* with its 21-gun salute. Goose bumps every time.

Hill adjacent to Iwo Jima Memorial, beneath Netherlands Carillon Memorial Pkwy., 0.2 mile south of Rosslyn Metro Station

HERE ARE MORE GOLD-MEDAL PLACES TO SPREAD A PICNIC AND WATCH THE SHOW

Note: You should arrive very early to secure a spot.

Air Force Memorial
Rising on a hill near the Pentagon, the Air Force Memorial provides a perfect fireworks vantage.

Gravelly Point
Just north of DCA on the George Washington Memorial Parkway, there are a few picnic tables here and portable restrooms, plus plenty of grass to sprawl out on and admire the show.

Key Bridge
Linking Rosslyn with Georgetown, the Francis Scott Key Bridge is famed for its views of the Potomac River. You can stroll over from the Rosslyn Metro Station and enjoy standing room only for an otherwise excellent perch to watch the fireworks.

Long Bridge Park
With three athletic fields, there's plenty of space to spread a blanket and admire the fireworks. The park is located at the northern end of Crystal City, easily accessible from the Crystal City Metro Station.

Mount Vernon Trail
This paved trail winding along the Potomac River has fabulous views of DC's monumental skyline, making it an excellent spot from which to watch the fireworks. You'll want to ride your bike here or rent one.

HIT
A STREET FESTIVAL

Sometimes it's nice just to stroll through a neighborhood street festival, taking in the arts, music, food, and fun—and even run into neighbors you don't often see. And that's what Clarendon Day is, one of Arlington's biggest street festivals, with more than 10,000 people turning out in mid-October to enjoy local cuisine, craft beers, and wines; live concerts on the central stage; local arts and crafts; a large Kidszone; and more. It's also a chance to check in with local nonprofits and to shake hands with locals running for political office. The best part? It seems like the weather's always perfect and everyone's in a good mood.

Clarendon Metro Park and adjacent six blocks
(use 3100 Wilson Blvd. for your GPS address), Clarendon, 703-812-8881
clarendon.org/clarendon-day

BE SOCIALLY CONSCIOUS
AT BUSBOYS AND POETS

If you want to help make the world a better place, join like-minded people at Busboys and Poets in Shirlington. There's always something interesting and important going on at this community gathering place that provides a forum to explore cultural, political, intellectual, and social issues—including book discussions, lectures, weekly open-mic poetry nights, and an ongoing discussion series on race. One night may host ANC meetings, with jazz performances the next. Everyone is welcome.

Artist, activist, and restaurateur Andy Shallal founded Busboys and Poets in Washington, DC, in 2004 as a restaurant, bar, bookstore, coffee shop, and events venue. Now there are nine in the region, including—thankfully—Shirlington since 2007. This is also the place to come for a good meal (the menu features a global mix of dishes) or to meet friends for a cocktail. Whatever brings you there, you'll eventually be drawn into the bookstore, guaranteed.

4251 S Campbell Ave., Shirlington Village, 703-379-9757
busboysandpoets.com/locations/?location=shirlington&venue=shirlington

---

FUN FACT

B&P was named for Langston Hughes, the American poet who worked as a busboy at the Wardman Park Hotel in the 1920s before becoming a famous poet.

GET PHYSICAL
AT THE SYNETIC THEATER

You haven't seen anything like this. Performers at the Synetic Theater in Crystal City use movement, sound, and lighting to turn works by the likes of Shakespeare, Edgar Allan Poe, and Robert Louis Stevenson into mesmerizing, minimalistic, visual theatrics. Basically, they take away the text and put it into body language—dance, athleticism, high-energy acting—to the beat of riveting music. They also run summer camps for kids as well as workshops for adults (learn how to climb mountains that aren't there and change your age or physical attributes!).

1800 S Bell St., Crystal City, 703-824-8060 (ext. 117 for box office)
synetictheater.org

JAZZ IT UP
AT JAZZ FEST

Jam to the cool tunes of Rosslyn's ever popular jazz fest every September in Gateway Park. It's a fun afternoon filled with international sounds and rhythms of jazz, along with yard games, food trucks, pop-up bars, and tons of fun. Past headliners have included Galactic, a proud New Orleans–based quintet; Mwenso & the Shakes, a Harlem group composed of international immigrants; and the Groove Orchestra, a jazz ensemble led by DC native and multi-instrumentalist Samuel Prather. Whoever's playing, reservations are recommended— Gateway Park fills up fast!

Gateway Park, 1300 Langston Blvd., Rosslyn
Rosslyn Business Improvement District: 703-522-6628
rosslynva.org

RELAX WITH A PINT AND LIVE MUSIC
AT WESTOVER MARKET BEER GARDEN

Westover Market Beer Garden comes alive on good-weather nights with a local crowd enjoying live music, six beers on tap, and a barbecue-focused menu. Weekends especially, it's hard to find a seat among the rows of picnic tables as families, couples, and friends enjoy a bit of chill time.

Any other time, the attached market—one of the area's few remaining independent markets—will fill your grocery basket with locally made ice cream, wild salmon, and made-to-order sandwiches. The butcher shop always has fresh, humanely raised, non-GMO meat from local farms.

Oh, and then the beer. Little by little, beer displays have taken over the market's walls and shelves, dubbed far and wide as the "Great Wall of Beer" for its 550-plus varieties of domestic and foreign—microbrews, all.

5863 Washington Blvd., Westover Village, 703-536-5040
westovermarketbeergarden.com

TIP
If it's raining or snowing outside, you can always head to the Beer Haus inside the market. The neighborhood bar offers 10 beers on tap and a menu of locally sourced dishes—though no live music.

EXPLORE BALLSTON QUARTER

For the longest time, Ballston Mall was a fading, dated space with little more than an old Macy's, a gym, a movie theater, and a handful of other shops. In 2018, the whole place experienced a facelift. It was rebranded Ballston Quarter, and a shining indoor-outdoor space was added. It has since become a popular destination! There are sit-down restaurants showcasing the best local chefs (including Ted's Bulletin and True Food), and a lively food hall offering street tacos, gourmet doughnuts, and local craft brews.

You can come here for cooking classes, get a haircut, or watch a movie in the fancy armchair theater. You can also cheer on the Caps or Nats at a watch party (remember, the Caps practice at the public skating rink's MedStar Capitals Iceplex on the top floor; see page 74). Fun special events include immersive art installations (such as the one made of interactive, larger-than-life tops in July 2023); and the annual Quarterfest Crawl, a day of pop-up concerts, performances, and samples from dozens of neighborhood restaurants. Admittedly, the shopping still isn't the biggest draw, but at this point it doesn't really matter.

4238 Wilson Blvd., Ballston, 703-243-6346
ballstonquarter.com

CATCH A COMEDY ACT OR CULT FLICK
AT THE ARLINGTON DRAFTHOUSE

Where else can you enjoy a comfortable chair, sample tasty dishes off a versatile menu, drink beer, and watch a cult film one night, and on the next night, be thoroughly entertained by a nationally touring comic? The Arlington Drafthouse on Columbia Pike is a landmark in these parts. It has, after all, been around since the cinema boom period of the 1930s and 1940s (it's officially a "historic property"). Back then, it was called the Arlington Theater & Bowling Alley, which opened in 1940. The complex featured a 24-lane bowling alley, several department stores, and the Arlington Pharmacy. The first film shown here was *My Favorite Wife*, starring Cary Grant and Irene Dunne. Tickets were 25 cents. For years, it was known as the Arlington Cinema and Draft House and showed feature and lesser known films, with comedy acts woven in between. Alas, with the rise of streaming and digital content, they've had a harder time these days on the film side of things. Currently, some cult films, festivals, and local independent films are on the docket—but there's a full slate of comedians. Times change, but you can still have a fun evening here.

2903 Columbia Pike, 571-765-5904
arlingtondrafthouse.com

TIP

Although it isn't yet a historical legend, the Alamo Drafthouse Cinema in Crystal City has nine auditoriums, each one offering dine-in service including a full bar—all brought to your seat.

1660 Crystal Dr., 571-814-3776
drafthouse.com/dc-metro-area/theater/crystal-city

REVEL IN A CELESTIAL SHOW
AT THE DAVID M. BROWN PLANETARIUM

For more than 50 years, Arlingtonians have had the remarkable opportunity to travel the Milky Way from right here in town, at the David M. Brown Planetarium. Its state-of-the-art Digester 7 system transports you to the heavens at warp speed, with a variety of rotating shows, including perhaps *Stars, Stars, Stars*; *Human Spaceflight*; or *Looking at Earth from Orbit*. It's a small and intimate space, with a small admission fee and an emcee named Bill who banters and directs a Q&A.

1426 N Quincy St., next to Washington-Liberty High School campus
703-228-6070
apsva.us/planetarium

FACT
The planetarium is named for Yorktown High graduate and astronaut David M. Brown, who died in the catastrophic 2003 Space Shuttle *Columbia* explosion.

ENJOY GOOD, OLD-FASHIONED FAMILY FUN
AT THE ARLINGTON COUNTY FAIR

Hop on a carnival ride, watch a concert, get your face painted, eat fried Oreos and funnel cakes—Arlington's annual county fair has all the attractions of the best county fairs. This family extravaganza has descended on Thomas Jefferson Community Center for five days every August for more than 45 years, and admission is always free. And while it has all the expected features, there are some unexpected ones as well. How about axe throwing? A sensory hour, in which all loud noises and music are eliminated for one hour on one day, so fairgoers can enjoy the space without feeling overwhelmed? A beer and rosé garden? Bingoat, where you play bingo in a room surrounded by wandering goats? And a weekend foam party (whatever that is . . .)? You'll just have to go and check it out!

Thomas Jefferson Community Center, 3501 2nd St. S, 703-829-7471
arlingtoncountyfair.us

GLORY IN
THE FREE LUBBER RUN AMPHITHEATER CONCERT SERIES

Lubber Run in the Arlington Forest neighborhood is a really great park for lots of reasons: a bubbling creek, picnic tables, wandering woodsy paths, and a relatively brand-new community center. But one of the best reasons to visit Lubber Run is its stage. Since the first permanent stage was constructed in 1969, this tree-shaded retreat off US 50 has featured free performances ranging from big band and blues to soul and cabaret. Mind you, these aren't just Podunk musicians showing up to strut their stuff. There have been some big names here, including Eddie from Ohio and Richie Havens. Sometimes full-out musicals are performed; *Joseph and the Amazing Technicolor Dreamcoat* appeared in 2022. So, bring a picnic and some friends, and enjoy an amazing night of music under the stars. The series generally runs June through August on Fridays and Saturdays at 8 p.m. and Sundays at 11 a.m.

2nd St. N at N Columbus St., Arlington Forest, 703-228-1850
arlingtonva.us/government/programs/arts/programs/lubber-run

TIP
There's a small parking lot and it fills up fast, so get there early.

BE ZEN
AT CRYSTAL CITY WATER PARK

All of a sudden, the concrete jungle of Crystal City doesn't feel so off-putting anymore, and Crystal City Water Park is a prime reason why. This revamped urban park, sprinkled with decorative water features, benches, public art installations, and plenty of grass, features a live performance stage and a flowing water wall with an open-air raw and cocktail bar perched on top. But that's not all. Restaurant kiosks highlighting up-and-coming local, minority-, and women-owned businesses provide lots of yummy eating opportunities—including Queen Mother's, a famous local fried chicken joint; and Brij, a DC wine bar and café that uses some of its proceeds to help single mothers, the unhoused, and the LGBTQ community.

This is the place you'll want to go to hang out after a crazy day of work or on a Saturday afternoon to listen to live music, gather with friends or colleagues, and just chill. It's right near the VRE station and the Crystal City Connector path (leading to the Mount Vernon Trail), making it easily accessible.

1601 Crystal Dr., Crystal City, 703-412-9430
nlwaterpark.com

TAKE IN MONUMENTAL VISTAS
FROM THE VIEW OF DC

As we may have mentioned, one of the advantages of being in Arlington is that you're not in DC. All the better to zip up 31 flights in Rosslyn's tallest skyscraper to the View of DC, a 12,000-square-foot, ceiling-to-floor-windowed viewing platform that takes in one of the world's most monumental views. From this lofty perch, you can see the sparkly Potomac River far below and pick out all the famous monuments: the Washington, Jefferson, Lincoln, and more. The US Capitol snuggles in the background, while Georgetown's spires, Kennedy Center, and National Cathedral all take part in this stunning vista. But since it's a 360-degree viewing platform, it's not just about DC.

Make your way around, and you'll see planes taking off from DCA, the Air Force Memorial's silvery plumes, Arlington National Cemetery's somber tombstones—and, if you squint, you may make out JFK's eternal flame. Farther west, a row of high-rises is essentially the route of the Metro's Orange Line, proving that location near public transportation in a large city is everything.

A small stairway leads to the 32nd floor, where an open-air, cantilevered terrace has breathtaking views.

1201 Wilson Blvd., Rosslyn, 703-769-4690
theviewofdc.com

GROOVE TO THE MUSIC
AT THE COLUMBIA PIKE BLUES FESTIVAL

Arlington has lots of different festivals, but one of the most popular is this lively music fest on Columbia Pike, taking place every summer since 1995. Deemed "Arlington's best block party" by *Arlington Magazine* and the DC metro area's largest blues festival, the free, outdoor Columbia Pike Blues Festival always promises an amazing time with stand-out local and national headliners, family fun, craft beer and wine, and unique local vendors. It's a chance to kick up your heels and enjoy one of life's great summer experiences.

S Walter Reed Dr. from Columbia Pike to 9th St. S, 703-892-2776
columbia-pike.org

Met Park

SPORTS
AND RECREATION

GET FIT
ON THE SUPERBLY SCENIC MOUNT VERNON TRAIL

The Mount Vernon Trail, a stunning, 18-mile paved pathway meandering along the Potomac River between Rosslyn and Mount Vernon is one of Arlington's greatest gifts—at least for those who like to walk, run, and bike—because about four miles lies within our city boundaries (we won't tell if you go beyond). Especially on sunny warm weekends, runners, walkers, bikers, and inline skaters converge on the path and picnickers spread blankets along its grassy banks.

The trail starts (or ends, depending on how you look at it) at mile marker 17 near Theodore Roosevelt Island (see page 56). As you approach Roosevelt Bridge, prepare to enter the most scenic part of the entire trail where the Lincoln and Jefferson Memorials and Washington Monument rise in white-marble splendor across the river. In spring, the fluffy blooms of cherry blossoms create a pink-and-white border along the water's edge.

Beyond, you'll reach Gravelly Point (see page 65), where plane-spotters watch airplanes take off and land at nearby DCA. The Arlington section of the trail officially ends just beyond the airport, at Four Mile Run.

Along the Potomac River between Teddy Roosevelt Island
and Four Mile Run, 703-289-2500
nps.gov/gwmp/planyourvisit/mtvernontrail.htm

WATCH PRO CYCLISTS COMPETE
AT THE CLARENDON CUP

One weekend every year, typically in June, world-class cyclists convene on Clarendon to race their hearts out. Imagine this: it's a one-mile course, taking in five tight turns of the city streets (essentially circling the Clarendon Metro Stop). It's sooooo thrilling! You watch how the riders stick together in the peloton—shielding your eyes at the prospect of a crash. Anyone who can't keep up with the group gets left behind. Where else can you see such high-caliber racers so close-up?

Part of the Armed Forces Cycling Classic, the event includes one pro male and one pro female race within a whole weekend of events. There's a challenge bike ride that anyone can join, as well as kids bike races. You can either watch it—or race yourself. What fun!

Clarendon streets near the Metro stop, 202-966-0346
cyclingclassic.org

TRY TO FIND TEDDY
AT THEODORE ROOSEVELT ISLAND

This woodsy isle lies officially within DC's boundaries, but the only way to access it is from Arlington. So we're taking advantage of that connection to include Theodore Roosevelt Island in this book because it is such a fantastic place.

The island looked completely different in the 1800s. Then, a plantation estate existed here, owned by descendants of Founding Father George Mason IV and worked by enslaved laborers in the corn and cotton fields. The family was forced to sell in 1831 when Mason's bad investments caught up with him. During the Civil War, Union soldiers occupied the island, and it was used to billet free African American soldiers attached to the US Colored Troops.

In the 1930s, the National Park Service acquired the island and turned it back to forest as a way to honor the 26th president. Today, trails lace this natural haven, offering glimpses of the glistening Potomac River, Georgetown's spires, and the Kennedy Center through the trees. Birds sing, squirrels cavort, and deer rustle in the underbrush. In the middle of it all, a bust honors the island's namesake, Theodore Roosevelt, who loved the wilderness, and would have loved this urban isle, too.

In the Potomac River near Key Bridge, 703-289-2500
nps.gov/this/planyourvisit/directions.htm

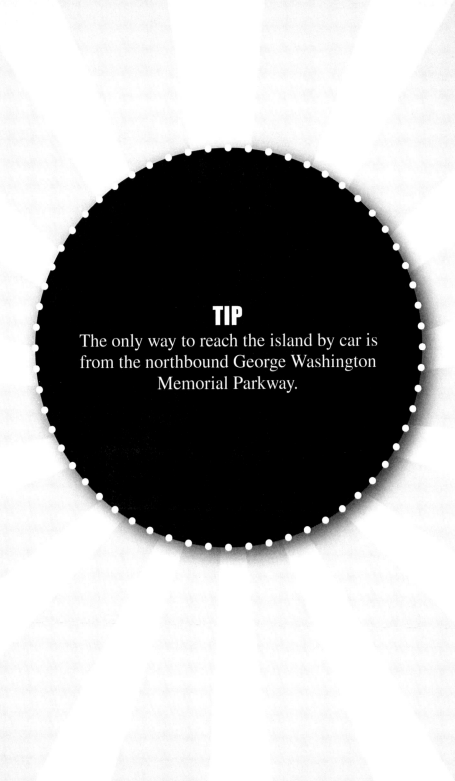

TIP
The only way to reach the island by car is from the northbound George Washington Memorial Parkway.

JUMP INTO THE POOL
AT THE LONG BRIDGE
AQUATICS & FITNESS CENTER

As one of the nation's fittest cities, Arlington has the inside track on swimming pools—*the* places to go for low-impact, cardiovascular workouts good for the entire body. Probably the best pool, the first-class Long Bridge Aquatics & Fitness Center, is run by the Arlington Aquatic Club—the county-run competitive swim program that helped train Olympic medalist Torri Huske and cost a whopping $60 million to build!

This expansive complex includes a pool for serious swimmers such as water polo players and synchronized swimmers and one for recreational swimmers, including lap lanes, a water slide, a lazy river, and a spa. Classes are offered and an 8,000-square-foot fitness center, lighted multisport fields, public art displays, a rain garden, and walking trails are all part of the package. The daily admission is a little pricey, but check out the different passes for better deals if you visit often.

333 Long Bridge Dr. near Crystal City, 703-228-3338
arlingtonva.us/government/departments/parks-recreation/locations/
indoor-facilities/long-bridge-aquatics-fitness-center

HERE ARE THREE BEAUTIFUL AQUATIC CENTERS AT LOCAL HIGH SCHOOLS THAT OFFER PUBLIC SWIMMING HOURS

Wakefield Aquatics Center
1325 S Dinwiddie St., 703-228-2395

Washington-Liberty Aquatics Center
1301 N Stafford St., 703-228-6262

Yorktown Aquatics Center
5200 Yorktown Blvd., 703-228-8754

Additional info is available at Arlington Public School Pools:
apsva.us/aquatics/aps-pools

CATCH A COLLEGE BASEBALL GAME
AT TUCKER FIELD

Yes, it's great to go see the Nationals play at Nats Park in DC, but you can still catch some high-caliber ball without crossing a bridge, dealing with the crowds, or paying the hefty ticket prices. Tucker Field at Barcroft Park, near Shirlington, is the home of the George Washington University baseball team, and was recently renovated to become one of the region's top collegiate facilities. The Colonials play all their home games here, and there's not a bad seat in the house. The complex comprises a press box, concession area, bullpens, enclosed dugouts, scoreboard, clubhouse, and seats for 500 spectators. You'll become a fan in no time. Find the Colonials' schedule at gwsports.com.

4200 S Four Mile Run Dr., near Shirlington, 703-228-4747
arlingtonva.us/government/departments/parks-recreation/
locations/parks/barcroft-park

TIP
The park also has tennis and basketball courts, an amazing playground, picnic areas, and trails and open spaces.

· ·

RIP OUT
INVASIVE PLANTS

Plants such as Bell's honeysuckle, the common daylily, and ground ivy may sound like innocuous—and even pleasant—plants. But in Arlington, they are not. They're dangerous invaders that have been introduced into the local ecosystem. They disrupt the ecology by displacing indigenous species that may not have developed defenses, introducing disease and inhibiting the growth and regeneration of native trees (among other nasty things).

But you can help do something about it. You can join Remove Invasive Plants (RIP) volunteers to help tear out the invasive plants. All you need to do is preregister online and check out the 10 different sites where workdays are regularly held.

Throughout Arlington, 703-228-1862
arlingtonva.us/government/programs/sustainability-and-environment/
trees/invasive-plants

UNCOVER STARTLING HISTORY
AT METROPOLITAN PARK

It's old news that Amazon is planting its second headquarters in Arlington, and little by little this megacompany is opening its doors in the newly rebranded National Landing (essentially staking out land in Crystal City and Pentagon City). They want to be part of the community and so are promising all kinds of welcoming venues, including restaurants, shops, and public spaces.

One of the most stunning elements is Metropolitan Park, a 2.5-acre green space edged by locally owned small businesses (including Toby's Homemade Ice Cream!). There's a dog park here, a fantastic children's park, a community garden with picnic tables and umbrella-shaded chairs for reading, and a native-tree-shaded central park with footpaths and places to rest. This latter space also features local art installations—you've got to love the whimsical, stainless-steel artworks by Iñigo Manglano-Ovalle depicting *Untitled Perched Objects* and displayed atop slim poles, such as a balancing umbrella and a disposable cup with its lid and straw weighted by its contents.

But pride of place is ceded to the absolute standout, *Queen City* (2023), a brick-tower monument by artist and DC resident Nekisha Durrett, located in the heart of the park. The use of brick harkens back to the area's past as a hub for brick production. Inside, bright blue ceramic vessels are suspended, each resembling a giant teardrop, to memorialize the 903 African Americans who were forced out of their homes in a neighborhood called Queen City when the Pentagon was built. This was accomplished with only nominal compensation (if at all) through eminent domain in 1942. It's a place of historical friction, in the face of today's accusations against Amazon for gentrifying the neighborhood and pricing people out. It makes us aware of what we shouldn't forget.

1400 S Eads St., Pentagon City/National Landing
queencityva.art

TIP

For visitor info, go to stayarlington.com or call 800-677-6267.

• •

ENJOY A TRADITIONAL CAMPFIRE WITH S'MORES
AT LONG BRANCH NATURE CENTER

The campfire stokes up and the air fills with smoky goodness, as the crickets chirp and stars gleam overhead. For every good reason you'd think you were deep in the wilderness and not in the heart of Arlington. But here you are, in a wooded retreat off Carlin Springs, at Long Branch Nature Center at Glencarlyn Park. On certain evenings, visitors are treated to storytelling, special animal guests, games, songs, and s'mores around a campfire—especially popular with families. (It's a well-attended event, so be sure to reserve ahead on the website.)

625 S Carlin Springs Rd., 703-228-6535
arlingtonva.us/government/departments/parks-recreation/locations/
nature-centers/long-branch-nature-center?lang_update=637738745849323354

TIP
During the day, the park offers hiking trails along a rocky stream and into the woods; a small nature center with turtles, snakes, and other live animals; a pond filled with belching frogs and dragonflies; and other refreshing doses of pure nature.

SPOT PLANES
AT GRAVELLY POINT

There's something mesmerizing about Gravelly Point. First of all, its location is stunning. Its grassy expanse overlooks the Potomac River and DC's marble-clad monuments, drawing families and groups of friends to picnic, play ball, hang out, and enjoy a pleasant afternoon. The Mount Vernon Trail (see page 54) laces through, making it accessible to bikers and runners. On nice days, there are even food trucks here.

But then, the air overhead fills with a mechanical clatter as a looming shadow moves across the ground, and everyone looks up at the sky as an enormous jet soars above, coming in for a landing at nearby Reagan Washington National Airport. The aluminum beast is so close you can feel the engine's rumble reverberate through your body and its underbelly shines. It makes a landing at the airport, and within minutes, another one is on its way. People watch in awe.

Gravelly Point Park, George Washington Memorial Pkwy.
(accessible from northbound lane only), 703-289-2500
nps.gov/places/000/gravelly-point.htm

TIP
Planes landing from the north fly in low and are more exciting to watch than those that land from the south, which fly much higher overhead.

LOSE YOURSELF TO WONDER
IN A PARK

Arlington has 184 parks. That's right—184 grassy, tree-filled retreats! Here's an amazing fact: 99 percent of Arlingtonians live within a 10-minute walk of a park. No wonder the Arlington park system is constantly ranked at the top of the list in the US (third in 2022). Some parks are big, some are small, some are tiny. Some parks are full of trees, others have playgrounds, while still others have recreational facilities, and some of the really special ones we've described in further detail elsewhere. There are so many things you can do in the parks:

- Walk your dog.
- Have a picnic.
- Take a nap.
- Bring your kids to the ones with playgrounds.
- Sit on a bench and breathe in the fresh air.
- Play basketball or sand volleyball or baseball.
- Cook out (many have grills).
- Run your toes through the grass.
- Observe birds, turtles, frogs, and salamanders.

What are you waiting for?

703-228-4747
arlingtonva.us/government/departments/parks-recreation

RUN
THE ARMY TEN-MILER

You're standing in a crowd of more than 35,000 runners outside the Pentagon, watching the famous Golden Knights—Army parachuters—appear as specks in the sky. The crowd erupts as the jumpers crystallize and land on a target right outside the Pentagon, and the race is on. This enormous gathering of runners, with all its fanfare, has taken place annually since 1985, and it remains one of Arlington's biggest road races. It also ranks as the world's second largest ten-mile road race. Yes, part of the course crosses into DC, but the beginning and glorious end are in Arlington, at the Pentagon. As you cross the finish line, you'll receive your participant medal and enjoy postrace fun, including music and food. There's also a youth run and a fun expo.

Begins and ends at the Pentagon, 202-997-6906
armytenmiler.com

TIP

If you want to race, sign up early (generally in March); it fills up fast.

JOIN
THE PICKLEBALL RAGE

Pickleball is the national rage, and Arlington is no different. There's a tough crew of pickleballers who show up at the courts religiously. But that doesn't mean beginners can't make a foray into the fun as well. Right now, there are several courts—essentially tennis courts where lines have been painted to show the pickleball court dimensions—where you can play pickleball. They include Fort Scott Park, Glebe Road Park, Gunston Park, Lubber Run Park (indoor and outdoor), and Walter Reed Park.

Word on the street is that, for beginners, Lubber Run is best, whereas the folks at Walter Reed Park don't look kindly upon the less experienced.

When you arrive, reserve your turn by placing your paddle in the paddle rack to indicate who plays next. When it's your turn, retrieve your paddle and go to the open court. You will play one game, to 11 points with a win by two, or 15 minutes if not playing a game. If you want to play another game, place your paddle in the next available slot in the paddle rack and repeat. So much fun!

Check the Arlington Government website (arlingtonva.us) for updates.

PLAY A ROUND OF DISC GOLF
IN BLUEMONT PARK

There's golf, and then there's disc golf. And Arlington is lucky enough to have a disc golf course that's ranked as one of Virginia's best. Located in Bluemont Park, it incorporates a hillside; the small, winding Four Mile Run; a grove of trees; and interesting natural landmarks such as a gnarled tree protecting a basket. Therefore, on this challenging course, you will be throwing uphill, downhill, across a valley, out of a chute, and through a stand of trees. Every hole has four tees and four pin placements—which some complain is a bit much, but what else can you do in a tight valley? Built in 1980, the course is one of the earliest, but it's been kept in great shape and serves players of all ages.

601 N Manchester St. in Bluemont Park, 703-228-4747
arlingtonva.us/government/departments/parks-recreation/locations/
parks/bluemont-park

STOP AND SMELL THE ROSES
AT BON AIR PARK

A trove of rosebushes blooms in a frenzy of color and aroma in mid-June in this special little garden in the Bon Air neighborhood. There are more than 3,000 rose plants and more than 120 different varieties. Benches sprinkled throughout provide the perfect rose-viewing perches.

It all started after World War II, when Arlingtonian Nellie Broyhill saw a *Time* magazine article talking about how cities across the nation were paying tribute to their troops with living memorials. An avid gardener herself, she created the Arlington Rose Garden Foundation to honor war veterans (including her son). She negotiated (and survived) the bureaucracy, and the garden was dedicated in 1951. There's a bench dedicated to her, next to a stone plaque that commemorates the 841 Arlingtonians who fought in the war.

You can reserve the space for weddings and other special events—talk about a divine venue! But most of all, simply stop by on a random afternoon, whether it's mid-June or not, and enjoy a few moments in this gloriously aromatic place. It will revive you.

850 N Lexington St., 703-371-9351
arlingtonva.us/government/departments/parks-recreation/locations/
parks/bon-air-park

TIP
The park also features a hillside that transforms into clouds of pink, purple, and white blooming azaleas in April.

TAKE A VACAY WITHOUT LEAVING ARLINGTON
AT ISLAND TIME BAR & GRILL

If you're yearning for a vacation vibe but don't have the time to drive to the shore, head to Columbia Island Marina. This tucked-away boat harbor may very well be Arlington's greatest secret. Here you will find picnic tables along the water, a disc golf course, and plenty of grass to toss down a blanket and take in some sun.

But what's most surprising is the presence of Island Time Bar & Grill. Outdoor seating overlooking the boats (and the Pentagon in the distance) provides the perfect low-key perch to feel the cool watery breezes while sipping a froufrou pineapple crush and eating crispy shrimp. Live music fills the air on weekends. Life is good.

Columbia Island, off southbound George Washington Memorial Pkwy.
near DCA, 202-347-0174, 202-347-0173 (Island Time)
boatingindc.com/marinas/columbia-island-marina

TIP
A short paved trail connects the island to the larger Mount Vernon Trail. It's the perfect stop on a long bike ride!

PEDAL
THE WASHINGTON AND OLD DOMINION TRAIL

Arlington always ranks as one of the nation's fittest cities, and this marvelous paved trail, running for 45 miles between Shirlington and Purcellville in Loudoun County, may very well explain why. The first five miles or so are in Arlington and on good weather days, especially weekends, it's populated by runners, bikers, walkers, dog walkers, and parents pushing baby strollers, all out stretching their legs. Time your workout carefully because it's also a major bike commuter route during morning and afternoon rush hour.

But it's not just about the exercise. Along the way, you will be treated to a dose of natural beauty that's surprising for the middle of the city. There are community gardens, copses of trees, and gurgling brooks along with bunnies, all kinds of birds, and deer (sometimes even majestic bucks). And, more importantly, you'll find water stops along the way.

The trail follows the old route of the regional Washington and Old Dominion Railroad, whose last passenger hopped aboard in 1951. The empty track limped along until 1979, when it was converted into this amazing recreational trail. Lucky us!

The Arlington portion lies between Shirlington and East Falls Church; the trailhead is at Shirlington Rd. and S Four Mile Run Dr. near Shirlington, 703-729-0596
novaparks.com/parks/washington-and-old-dominion-railroad-regional-park

WATCH YOUR FAVORITE CAPS PLAYERS PRACTICE
AT THE MEDSTAR CAPITALS ICEPLEX

No need to trek all the way into DC to watch your favorite Caps at the Capital One Arena. Ovechkin and other Stanley Cup–winning Washington Capitals hockey players practice at their official home, the MedStar Capitals Iceplex, located on the top floor of the Ballston Quarter parking garage. And their practices are open to the public—for free!

The complex features two NHL-size, state-of-the-art ice rinks, a full-service pro shop, and a team store with Caps apparel, jerseys, mugs, and more. Check out their schedule at nhl.com/capitals/team/practice.

Wait around after, and you may get to meet some of the superstars. And the cool thing is, you can skate here too (but not when the Caps are practicing, of course). You can also take figure-skating and hockey lessons.

627 N Glebe Rd. in Ballston Quarter, 571-224-0555
medstarcapitalsiceplex.com

STROLL THROUGH VIRGINIA WOODLANDS
AT POTOMAC OVERLOOK REGIONAL PARK

You don't expect expansive woodlands in the middle of urbanity, but there it is: the 70-acre Potomac Overlook Regional Park just off Military Road in North Arlington. An easy, rolling, 1.6-mile loop traverses these gorgeous Virginia woods: oaks, beech, and tulip poplars, especially splendid in autumn and spring. Robins, white-throated sparrows, and tufted titmice flit about; downy woodpeckers jab at tree trunks; and squirrels rustle through the brush, providing an extraordinary dose of nature.

An on-site nature center has interactive exhibits on local flora and fauna, plus several non-releasable birds of prey. There are also native plant gardens and an organic vegetable garden, and the park also hosts a summer outdoor concert series that draws families and friends.

2845 N Marcey Rd., 703-528-5406
novaparks.com/parks/potomac-overlook-regional-park

BIKE
THE ARLINGTON LOOP

Arlington is blessed with numerous paved trails. And if you need one little insight into how important they are to Arlingtonians, just consider the fact they're often cleared of snow before the streets are. Although Arlington has many stellar trails, serious bikers know about the Arlington Loop, a 16-mile loop of four paved, vehicle-free trails through central and southern Arlington (Washington & Old Dominion, Custis, Mount Vernon, and Four Mile Run). You can take these routes to almost anywhere in Arlington. Along the way, you'll see the sparkling Potomac River, with gold-medal views of the white-marble monuments (Mount Vernon); Sparrow Pond, with an overlook to view turtles, bullfrogs, and beavers (W&OD); Gravelly Point, where planes fly just overhead on their final descent to DCA (Mount Vernon); and a babbling creek (Four Mile Run). In Rosslyn, wave to the Bikeometer, an electronic device that keeps daily and monthly tallies of bikers.

Multiple entry locations, 703-786-3491
bikearlington.com/the-arlington-loop-a-community-gem/?fbclid=iwar3nuh wg5fyhkvrwjimfvjcentflppvf6v3s46ud6ujbaayzef-dbf3ukcw

---

TIP
Warning: The hills along the Custis coming from Rosslyn are brutal!

CLIMB UPTON

Sometimes you just have to give in to good, old-fashioned fun, and Upton Hill Regional Park provides plenty of ways to do that. This regional park is the closest thing Arlington has to an amusement park, after all. There are serious fast-pitch batting cages, an 18-hole mini golf course, and a fabulous water park, including several pools, two huge slides, and a big bucket that dumps water.

But most impressive of all is the aerial ropes climbing course, with easy, medium, and hard levels of climbs. Rising 40 feet off the ground, it has 90 built-in elements on three levels, including zip lines, a zip sled, tunnels, ladders, a surfboard, a cargo net, and a "hanging picnic table" at the tippy top (don't worry—harnesses and helmets are mandatory). It's a bit pricey, but the heart-pounding thrills make it worthwhile.

6060 Wilson Blvd., 703-534-3437
novaparks.com/parks/upton-hill-regional-park

TIP
Here, too, a 0.8-mile loop trail explores one of the last remaining forests in the Seven Corners area.

ACT LIKE A TOURIST
ALONG THE GEORGE WASHINGTON MEMORIAL PARKWAY

Imagine a beautiful roadway snaking along a glittering river, shaded by blooming trees and offering views of some of the nation's most famous monuments. It's not a figment of the imagination—this is the George Washington Memorial Parkway, a National Park Service–run byway that meanders 25 miles between Mount Vernon and I-495. Arlington claims about eight of those stunning miles, between Four Mile Run and Pimmit Run.

And yes, there are spectacular, drop-dead-gorgeous views across the Potomac to DC's monuments along the way (please keep your eye on the road!). But don't forget Arlington's highlights too, including Theodore Roosevelt Island (see page 56), Gravelly Point (see page 65), and the Lyndon Baines Johnson Memorial Grove (see page 80).

Pack a picnic, take a slow drive, and find a spot to stop and enjoy. Your options are plentiful.

Along the Potomac River between Mount Vernon and I-495
703-289-2500
nps.gov/gwmp/index.htm

ENJOY THE GOOD LIFE
AT GATEWAY PARK

The best of Arlington life unfurls at this urban park in Rosslyn: outdoor movie nights, fitness classes, and the Rosslyn Jazz Fest in September. There's also a dog park and sandbox for kids (the largest in Arlington), and locals know it's one of the best places to catch the DC Fourth of July fireworks. But it's also a place to just sit on the grass and soak up the rays or read a book, or traverse the meandering walkway past trees, shrubs, and flowers. Whenever you need a break from life's frantic pace, this is the place.

1300 Langston Blvd., Rosslyn, 703-228-4747
arlingtonva.us/government/departments/parks-recreation/locations/
parks/gateway-park

WALK THROUGH A BEAUTIFUL GROVE OF TREES HIDDEN IN PLAIN SIGHT
AT LBJ MEMORIAL GROVE

Literally steps from the George Washington Memorial Parkway just north of DCA, you'll find a peaceful natural world of oaks, tulip poplars, hollies, and white pines laced with serpentine paths. This is the Lyndon Baines Johnson Memorial Grove on the Potomac, dedicated to the 36th president of the United States, who loved nature and the outdoors. He used to come here when he needed a place to escape the stresses of the world, and so his wife, Lady Bird, chose it as the place for his memorial. There are benches and picnic areas for relaxing and enjoying a splash of nature. In the center, a granite monolith honors President Johnson and his achievements in civil rights, social reforms, and public service during the turbulent '60s. It's hard to imagine this quiet beauty resides so close to civilization. And yet there it is, waiting for us to embrace it, just as President Johnson once did.

Approach via the southbound lanes of the GW Parkway, north of DCA, or from Boundary Channel Drive at the Pentagon, where a wooden bridge takes you across Boundary Channel to the grove.
nps.gov/lyba/index.htm

TIP
The Mount Vernon Trail passes by the park; follow signs on the trail to pass beneath the parkway at Humpback Bridge and into the parking lot.

SPOIL FIDO
AT SHIRLINGTON DOG PARK

Where would we be without our dogs? A lot lonelier, that's for sure. So, we need to spoil our best friends. Lucky for us, Arlington has 10 county-sanctioned dog parks, where pups can cavort, run off-leash, meet other dogs, and sniff away to their hearts' content. Having such places for our pets truly fills our hearts with joy.

All the parks are good, but if dogs could vote, they'd probably raise their paws for Shirlington Dog Park. It's a huge, narrow space, about a quarter mile long, with a separate area for smaller dogs. And there are always lots of dogs, making it a primo yappy hour. Dogs can also access Four Mile Run to splash and cool off on steamy days, though some say the water isn't too clean (they generally let you know if it may not be safe).

2710 S Oakland St., Shirlington Village, 703-228-6525
arlingtonva.us/government/departments/parks-recreation/locations/
parks/shirlington-park/shirlington-dog-park

HERE ARE SOME OTHER DOG PARKS

Benjamin Banneker Park
1680 N Sycamore St.

Fort Barnard Dog Park
2101 S Pollard St.

Fort Ethan Allen Dog Park
3829 N Stafford St.

Gateway Interim Dog Park
1300 Langston Blvd.

Glencarlyn Dog Park
301 S Harrington St.

James Hunter Dog Park
1230 N Hartford St.

Towers Dog Park
801 S Scott St.

Utah Dog Park
3191 S Utah St.

Virginia Highlands Interim Dog Park
1600 S Hayes St.

Visit arlingtonva.us/government/departments/parks-recreation/
locations/dog-parks for more info about Arlington's dog parks.

Iwo Jima Memorial

MEXICO 1846-1848 ★ WAR BETWEEN THE STATES 1861-1865 ★ SPANISH WAR 1898 ★
★ LEBANON 1958 ★ VIET NAM 1962-1975 ★ DOMINICAN · REPUBLIC

CULTURE
AND HISTORY

GO ON A TREASURE HUNT
FOR THE NATION'S FIRST FEDERAL MONUMENTS

You've probably seen them a million times, without really registering their worn-down, eroded shape. Hidden in plain sight, a scattering of stone markers appears around Arlington. They might not look like much, but these are boundary stones—the nation's oldest federal monuments, actually—marking the original boundary of the District of Columbia. Each one is etched with the date it was installed (1791 for Virginia or 1792 for Maryland) plus a few other things, including the magnetic compass variance at that place. You'll find them beneath a water tower, in the middle of a road median, in several parks, in someone's backyard (knock and ask politely if you want to see it), and more.

Spearheaded by President George Washington, Benjamin Banneker and Andrew Ellicott charted the district's outline—a 100-square-mile diamond shape—with 40 markers distanced one mile apart, and eight are in Arlington.

Wait, what? Arlington? Arlington's not part of DC, right?

Actually, back in the earliest days it was, when in 1801 the land that includes present-day Arlington County and Alexandria City was ceded to the federal government to become part of the new national capital. But in 1847, the land was retroceded back to Virginia (the state's proslavery sentiments were part of the consideration among lawmakers).

The markers remain, housed in Victorian-era cages, as reminders of this fascinating history. They make a really fun treasure hunt, whether by bike or by car. You can learn more and get the location of each one at boundarystones.org.

ARLINGTON'S BOUNDARY STONES

Southwest 4
On the east side of King St. between Wakefield and the entrance to I-395

Southwest 5
North side of Walter Reed Pkwy., just east of intersection with King St.

Southwest 6
Median strip of Jefferson St., .01 mile south of Columbia Pike

Southwest 7
5995 S 5th Rd.

Southwest 8
100 feet southeast of the water tower behind the Patrick Henry Apartments, near the intersection of John Marshall Dr. and Wilson Blvd.

Northwest 1
3607 Powhatan St.

Northwest 2
5298 Old Dominion Dr./5145 N 38th St.

Northwest 3
4013 N Tazewell St.

• •

TAKE A WALK THROUGH ARLINGTON'S DARK HISTORY
IN HALLS HILL

Sometimes we don't realize how history affects us, but even in our own backyards it can come back to haunt us. Parts of a seven-foot-tall cinder-block wall built in the 1930s to separate Black Arlingtonians from white Arlingtonians, for example, still remain in the Halls Hill neighborhood, a poignant reminder of segregation's enduring legacy of hate.

The land in North Arlington originally belonged to an infamously vicious slaveowner, Basil Hall, who fled when the Civil War arrived on his doorstep in 1861. After the war, the property value dropped, and in 1881, Hall sold plots at a cheap rate, many to formerly enslaved individuals. The community became known as Halls Hill.

In the 1930s, a new neighborhood called Woodlawn was constructed, and that's when the "segregation wall" was built, to keep the Halls Hill citizens out. Halls Hill and adjoining Hyde View Park became a thriving, self-sufficient community with restaurants, businesses, and services. The African American residents even created their own fire department, since the local firehouse wouldn't serve them.

Larger sections of the wall were removed in 1966, and a flash flood destroyed more of it. Today, a historical marker stands near the intersection of North Culpeper Street and 17th Road North, recalling this horrific history.

History walking tours are offered of Halls Hill, taking in Fire Station 8, the first Black-staffed fire station south of the Mason-Dixon Line (which recently was completely and gloriously rebuilt); the John M. Langston Mural, paying tribute to Virginia's first Black congressman (1890–1891); and Calloway Cemetery, where freed enslaved people were laid to rest in the 19th century.

Historical marker
Intersection of N Culpeper St. and 17th Rd. N,
in the Waycroft-Woodlawn neighborhood

Fire Station 8
4845 Langston Blvd.

John M. Langston Mural
5010 Langston Blvd.

Calloway Cemetery
5000 Langston Blvd.

hallshill.com

• •

DISCOVER THE ARLINGTON CEMETERY
THAT TOURISTS DON'T KNOW

As Arlingtonians, we have taken our fair share of out-of-towners to visit this esteemed cemetery (so often we could probably lead the tour ourselves!). Granted, the sanctity of the place never gets old, as, in hushed reverence, we wander around the more than 400,000 white tombstones that sprinkle green hillsides across 639 sacred acres. There's Joe Louis Barrow's tomb, the world-champion boxer who served in World War II; Dr. Anita Newcomb, the first female surgeon in the US Army; and explorer Robert Peary, a former naval officer who is credited with discovering the geographic North Pole, just to name a few. JFK and Jackie's graves are located that way, and the Changing of the Guard, with its amazingly precise sentinels, occurs in the other direction.

All that said, there are unique ways to experience the cemetery that aren't on the typical tourist trail, ways that truly make you stop and think. On National Wreaths Across America Day, for example, you can help place Christmas wreaths on the headstones in a somber tribute to those who gave the greatest sacrifice. (To participate, you need to register ahead of time on the cemetery's website.)

Another special time is Easter, when the Memorial Amphitheater hosts a sunrise service featuring the music of the US Army Band. It's first come, first served, so you may have to pry yourself out of bed extra early that day—but if you're keen to attend a nondenominational Christian service, it's worth it to see the sun rising into the sky in this hallowed space.

1 Memorial Dr., 877-907-8585
arlingtoncemetery.mil

EXPLORE THE UNDERBELLY OF DRUGS
AT THE DEA MUSEUM

No, we're not talking about doing drugs. We're talking about a museum that showcases the fascinating stories behind global drugs, and the work the Drug Enforcement Agency (DEA) has done around the world for the past 150 years to rout out illicit drug activity. Inside one of the nondescript buildings on Army Navy Drive in Pentagon City, you'll discover thrilling, interactive exhibits that delve into the science and history of opium, marijuana, and cocaine, while a rotating spotlight display showcases such noteworthy moments as "taking down El Chapo."

However, it's the artifacts that are most riveting. The DEA's collection of more than 5,000 objects and 40,000 photographs includes green platform shoes worn by a DEA special agent while investigating a 1970s cocaine ring; a poppy scraper used by farmers to score and drain raw opium from poppy pods; and the life mask made before the death of notorious drug trafficker Pablo Escobar, a leader of the Medellín Cartel. It's eye-opening, and terrifying at the same time.

700 Army Navy Dr., Pentagon City, 202-307-3463
museum.dea.gov

TIP

It's best to visit in person, but collection highlights can be viewed online at museum.dea.gov/museum-collection/collection-spotlight.

FIND YOUR FLOW
BY MAKING ART

Escaping into the world of art frees the heart and soul, providing one of the best ways to escape the hustle and bustle of everyday life. You know you're doing it right when you have no sense of what time it is or how many hours have passed because you're so engrossed in the creative process. Johann Hari, the author of *Stolen Focus*, calls this escape the flow state. He writes: "It is the deepest form of focus and attention that we know of. . . . The more we achieve flow, the happier and healthier we'll be." Of course, you can find your flow dancing or running or writing, but art is one of the best ways. Lucky for us, Arlington has several different art centers where we can find our artistic flow.

Arlington Arts Center

Year-round art classes for novice and experienced artists, including drawing, painting, mixed media, and printmaking.
3550 Wilson Blvd., 703-248-6800
arlingtonartscenter.org/education

Art House 7

Ceramics, sculpture, drawing, painting, and sewing are some of the classes available for ages 4 to adult in this comfortable, two-story studio on Langston Boulevard.
5537 Langston Blvd., 703-269-0946
arthouseseven.com

Fairlington Art Studios

Classes, workshops, and art camps.
Fairlington Community Center
3308 S Stafford St., 703-228-6588
arlingtonva.us/government/departments/parks-recreation/
locations/indoor-facilities/fairlington-community-center-park

Muse Paint Bar

Paint a beautiful painting—and enjoy beer, wine, and tasty bites while you are at it.
Ballston Quarter, 4238 Wilson Blvd., 888-607-6873
musepaintbar.com/events/arlington-paint-bar

VISIT ARLINGTON'S OLDEST HOUSE
AT THE BALL-SELLERS HOUSE

After all these years, the Ball-Sellers house still stands on Third Street South in the Glencarlyn neighborhood, providing a glimpse into how average folks lived back in the 1750s—as opposed to George Washington's Mount Vernon, which is our main point of reference for that time period. The one-room farmhouse, which originally belonged to John Ball and his family, is tiny but pretty interesting, with its original plank floors, archaeological tidbits uncovered during various digs, and the rustic loft where five Ball daughters slept. A painting of John Ball building his cabin by Rudy Wendelin (who incidentally was the first to draw Smokey Bear; he lived in nearby Bluemont) showcases the house's original frontier log structure in a woodsy setting. After Ball died in 1766, William Carlin bought the place—he was George Washington's tailor—and it's mind-boggling to think the future first president might have stopped by when he was surveying his nearby forestlands (see page 112). Not quite the Mount Vernon he was used to!

5620 3rd St. S, Glencarlyn, 703-577-7042
arlingtonhistoricalsociety.org/visit/ball-sellers-house

SURVEY THE GOINGS-ON
AT KEY BRIDGE

There's more to Francis Scott Key Bridge than meets the eye. Connecting Georgetown with Rosslyn, the concrete arch bridge opened on January 17, 1923, making it the region's oldest surviving road bridge spanning the Potomac River. Designed in Classic Revival style, it's named for Francis Scott Key, author of the "Star-Spangled Banner," who lived just on the opposite side in Georgetown. His house is no longer there, but a little park at the bridge's Georgetown entrance honors Key.

While it's often choked by traffic, the bridge is a glorious place to stroll, taking in sparkling river views, kayakers, Theodore Roosevelt Island, and Georgetown University's spires. Sunset is spectacular. It's also a primo spot to watch the Fourth of July fireworks over the National Mall.

Key Bridge
Over the Potomac River between Rosslyn and Georgetown

TIP

Here are two sources for additional information:

StayArlington
800-677-6267
stayarlington.com

DC Historic Sites
historicsites.dcpreservation.org/
items/show/311

VISIT *DARK STAR PARK*
ON AUGUST 1

Every year on August 1, at precisely 9:32 a.m., a crowd gathers at a traffic island in Rosslyn around two concrete balls and metal poles. At exactly the right moment, the crowd gasps and claps as the light aligns just right so that the shadows of the spheres and poles match with permanent shadow-images in the ground. This celestial spectacle is the 1984 work of artist Nancy Holt, who was part of the earth, land, and conceptual art movements and devoted to finding new places where art could be found. Well, she found that here.

The public artwork is called *Dark Star Park* and within a little 0.4-acre space it comprises five large concrete balls in total, some positioned along the curb in addition to the ones on the traffic island, plus two pools, four steel poles, and two tunnels. It's truly something to partake in the gathering on its special day. The rest of the year, take time to meditate at this otherworldly art piece.

1655 N Fort Myer Dr., Rosslyn
arlingtonva.us/government/departments/parks-recreation/locations/
parks/dark-star-park

WATCH THE SUNSET
AT THE AIR FORCE MEMORIAL

Three silvery plumes soar gracefully into the blue sky, visible from far and wide. The Air Force Memorial, perched near Arlington National Cemetery overlooking the Pentagon, was built in 2006 to honor the men and women of the US Air Force. The stainless-steel spires recall the contrails of Air Force Thunderbirds as they disperse in a "bomb burst" maneuver. A missing fourth Thunderbird symbolizes the missing man formation used at Air Force military funerals.

There's more than just the stunning sculpture, however. Inscriptions on surrounding granite walls celebrate the heritage and valor of aviation pioneers, while a Glass Contemplation Wall pays tribute to fallen airmen and women.

At sunset, the western horizon takes on a pink and gold glow in what's got to be one of Arlington's most beautiful places to salute the end of the day. Stay here awhile and take it all in.

1 Air Force Memorial Dr. near Arlington National Cemetery, 240-612-0478
afdw.af.mil/afmemorial/?utm_source=washingtonorg&utm_
medium=referral

REMEMBER THE KIDS WHO PERISHED
IN THE 9/11 ATTACK ON THE PENTAGON

On September 11, 2001, after two jets struck the Twin Towers in New York City, American Airlines Flight 77 crashed into the Pentagon's west side, killing 184 people—64 passengers, crew, and hijackers aboard the hijacked jet and 125 Pentagon workers on the ground. Among the plane's passengers was a group of inner-city students and three DC public school teachers who were en route to California to visit Channel Islands National Park as part of a special National Geographic field trip.

They and the others who perished that day are remembered at the National 9/11 Pentagon Memorial, outside the Pentagon wall where the plane hit. Each victim is honored with an illuminated bench inscribed with his or her name, age, and location at the time of the attack. The memorial is open 24/7, and a 24-minute audio tour that leads you to points of interest is available by calling 202-741-1004. Needless to say, it's a somber space, and one that's important for educating future generations.

1 N Rotary Rd., 703-996-9853
pentagonmemorial.org

PICK A FEW HIGHLIGHTS
FROM ARLINGTON'S EXTENSIVE OUTDOOR ART GALLERY

Spanish artist Eva Salmerón once said: "Public art is for everybody, and it is shown in places where you are passing by . . . It's a spontaneous encounter, no prejudice, no expectations, a surprise. Something new that changes the landscape of the city."

That's the perfect way to describe the experience of coming across Arlington's more than 80 permanent public artworks—sculptures, murals, art installations, and more—that decorate sidewalks, walls, courtyards, and roadsides. These pieces are whimsical, meaningful, colorful, and/or just fun. You might spot some by accident—*Luminous Bodies* by Cliff Garten, located near Key Bridge in Rosslyn, is an obvious one, rising above one of the major entrances into Arlington from Washington, DC. The work comprises four sculptures enhanced with LED lighting, continually changing color.

You can also take a self-guided walking tour of 14 works offered by StayArlington (stayarlington.com/blog/discover-arlingtons-award-winning-public-art-on-an-intriguing-walking-tour). Or you can just walk around the city and keep your eyes open. What fun!

GET THE FULLER STORY
AT ARLINGTON HOUSE

For decades, Arlington House celebrated Robert E. Lee, who lived there for 30 years with his family until the Civil War. After much internal struggle, he resigned from the US Army on April 21, 1861, choosing to fight instead for the Confederacy. When he walked out of the house two days later to take his command, he never would return. His surrounding plantation was turned into Arlington National Cemetery, where some of the war's Union dead occupied the first burial sites.

Recently reopening after an extensive renovation, Arlington House today aims to tell the fuller story—not only of Lee and his mansion, but of the African Americans who were forced to live and work there as well. Perhaps most poignant about this new approach are the questions—some hard-hitting and thought-provoking—sprinkled on placards throughout the house, the former enslaved quarters now housing exhibits and films, and a small outlying museum focusing on Lee himself. Visitors are asked to consider things like: Do you think a government has an obligation to protect enemy property? How does the size of your home affect your family? In what ways do you struggle for freedom? How do we reconcile Lee's many roles as soldier, father, slaveholder, and educator? They are questions that will linger with you long after you leave.

Arlington National Cemetery, 1 Memorial Ave., 703-235-1530
nps.gov/arho

TAKE
A COOKING CLASS

Arlington doesn't have its own cuisine, per se, but what fun to learn how to cook the cuisine of other regions and countries! And there are plenty of opportunities to do that—the perfect idea for a date night, family night, and grandparent night. Here are some ideas:

Cookology in Ballston Quarter has classes that dive deep into French cooking, fine Caribbean, and—what fun—farmers market with mixology (dishes include eggs Florentine Benedict, Bloody Mary baked beans, and vanilla and peach Bellini).

Sur La Table in Pentagon City has a constant schedule of classes, ranging from French Elegance and Latin American Dining to Exploring Thai Flavors.

Cookology
4238 Wilson Blvd., 703-433-1909
cookologyonline.com

Sur La Table
1101 S Joyce St., Ste. B-20, 703-414-3580
surlatable.com/store-details?StoreID=24

GET THE SCOOP
ON ARLINGTON'S CIVIL WAR DEFENSES

As the Civil War raged in the 1860s, Arlington became a strategic last line of defense to protect the federal capital. The US Army constructed a series of earthworks in Arlington, Alexandria, and Washington, DC. Two forts in Arlington are worth a peek.

At Fort C.F. Smith Park, you'll find the ruins of a fort dating from 1863. It was built on the property of Thomas Jewell, who lived with his family until "the soldiers robbed my house and ordered me off." There's a bombproof, the fort well, the north magazine, and six of the 22 gun emplacements. A visitor center has displays on Civil War history, and kids can try on replica uniforms.

Fort Ethan Allen was built in 1861 to command all approaches to Chain Bridge. Its remains are located in what's now Fort Ethan Allen Park, including large earthworks and the fort's remaining interior structures.

The Arlington line was never attacked. Clear proof it was an effective defense system.

Fort C.F. Smith Park
2411 24th St. N, 703-228-4775 (Civil War Visitor Center)
arlingtonva.us/government/departments/parks-recreation/locations/
parks/fort-cf-smith-park

Fort Ethan Allen
3829 N Stafford St., 703-228-3831
arlingtonva.us/government/projects/project-types/local-historic-district/
fort-ethan-allen

CELEBRATE FEMALE WARRIORS
AT THE MILITARY WOMEN'S MEMORIAL

From outside, it looks like a neoclassical wall gracing the ceremonial entrance to Arlington National Cemetery. As beautiful as it is, it's more than just a wall. Step inside and you'll find interactive exhibits, an education center, and a theater that all tell the stories of military women through the ages—three million of whom have served since the Revolutionary War. Did you know that women worked as spies during the Revolutionary War and that others disguised themselves as men so they could serve in the military? Interesting facts like these are sprinkled throughout.

Do not leave without climbing to the roof to experience the 360-degree vista. Behind, Arlington's rows of snow-white tombstones march over the hillside, while in front, the Memorial Bridge and Lincoln Memorial unfurl in a star-studded DC view. Inspiring quotes are etched into glass panels, encouraging you to linger awhile.

Ceremonial entrance to Arlington National Cemetery
Memorial Ave. and Schley Dr., 703-533-1155
womensmemorial.org

LEARN SOMETHING NEW
AT ARLINGTON'S CENTRAL LIBRARY

The Arlington Library System has nine library branches, with Central Library being, naturally, the main one. It's a great place to go if you need to do some quiet work—no one will find you on the second floor, tucked behind the stacks. But each library also offers an exciting schedule of events and learning opportunities. You can practice Japanese, Spanish, or Chinese in a conversation class; attend a gardening talk; take your kids to family story time; and learn about 3D printing, just to name a few. And libraries are still the places to go to find your next good read!

1015 N Quincy St., 703-228-5990
library.arlingtonva.us/locations/central-library

PONDER THE PAST
AT THE BLACK HERITAGE MUSEUM OF ARLINGTON

It may be small, but this museum on Columbia Pike is jam-packed with photos, artifacts, and detailed captions that delve into Arlington's rich Black history in a giant way. The exhibits begin by describing the enslaved workers brought to Arlington House from Mount Vernon and the subsequent establishment of Freedom Village before and after the Civil War. "Freedman's Village is the heart and soul of Arlington," says Dr. Scott Taylor, the museum's president and director.

After the Civil War, more than 75 percent of Arlingtonians were African American—until the Jim Crow laws kicked in, and all that changed. A segregation wall was built in one neighborhood to keep Blacks out. A wall of photos and newspaper clippings depicts the first four Black kids to attend an integrated Arlington school, in 1959. More pictures show 1960s sit-ins in local drugstores.

Famous locals include singing diva Roberta Flack and Charles Drew, who invented blood plasma storage. Also learn about Selina Gray, who saved heirlooms from Arlington House during the Civil War; Joan Mulholland, a civil rights fighter who still stops by the museum, and others.

Check the website for special events.

3045B Columbia Pike, 703-271-8700
arlingtonblackheritage.org

DELVE INTO ARLINGTON'S ATTIC
AT THE ARLINGTON HISTORICAL MUSEUM

You probably have driven past this historic-school-cum-museum on South Arlington Ridge Road a million times without realizing the wealth of interesting info awaiting inside. Housed in the historic Hume School, the county's oldest existing schoolhouse (dating from 1891), the building is filled with artifacts telling Arlington's story, like a family attic stashed with decades and decades of memories from the past. It starts with the Native Americans and continues with the colonial period, Civil War, industrialization, World War II, the African American experience, the Pentagon, and 9/11, and it highlights the many ways our city has played a role in our nation's history. There are always rotating exhibits exploring something intriguing—recently, there was a presentation on the construction of DCA (aka Reagan Washington National Airport), with photos showing what the landscape looked like when the airport was small. A schoolroom has also been preserved to look as it did at the turn of the 20th century—you can even ring the school bell.

The museum also hosts lectures and other events at the museum and elsewhere (including on Zoom). It's a great way to study up on local history.

1805 S Arlington Ridge Rd., 703-892-4204
arlingtonhistoricalsociety.org

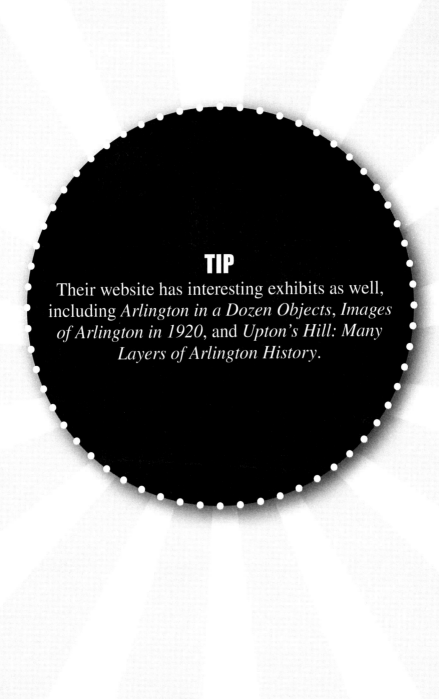

TIP

Their website has interesting exhibits as well, including *Arlington in a Dozen Objects, Images of Arlington in 1920*, and *Upton's Hill: Many Layers of Arlington History*.

BE CONTEMPORARY
AT MOCA ARLINGTON

A tucked-away historic school building on Wilson Boulevard houses the small but ambitious Museum of Contemporary Art Arlington (formerly Arlington Arts Center). Most of the exhibits in the nine galleries delve into local history and culture—whether it's a recent showing of Columbia Pike's documentary project, *A World in a Zip Code*, or the unforgettable *Reclining Liberty* by Zaq Landsberg sprawling on the museum's front lawn.

But there's more than meets the eye. A lively artist residency program is located here—with one gallery devoted to their works. And there are also lots of fun activities going on, whether it's Yoga in the Galleries, art-making classes, artist talks, or summer camp for kids.

3550 Wilson Blvd. in Virginia Square, 703-248-6800
mocaarlington.org

PICNIC
AT THE NETHERLANDS CARILLON

In the 1950s, the Dutch presented the American people with this carillon near Arlington National Cemetery to thank them for assistance provided during and after World War II. For the longest time, it didn't chime, but recently it was fixed. And while the chiming of the 53 bells is really nice, there are more reasons people come here. A bounty of tulips, fittingly, bloom in spring. A weekly concert series livens up summer evenings, featuring jazz, pop, and other musical styles, and the bells are programmed to play patriotic music daily at noon and 6 p.m., including "The Star-Spangled Banner" and the Dutch national anthem.

But perhaps the most amazing thing is the grassy knoll upon which it's located, providing an iconic view of the nation's capital, with the Lincoln Memorial, Washington Monument, and US Capitol lined up in a row. It's a popular place for picnics, most notably on the Fourth of July, when you need to arrive very early to stake your spot on the grass. It could very well be the best seat in the nation for the annual fireworks spectacle.

N Marshall Dr., Fort Myer, 703-289-2500
nps.gov/gwmp/learn/historyculture/netherlandscarillon.htm

DISCOVER
GEORGE WASHINGTON'S ARLINGTON FOREST

Everyone knows the nation's first president lived at Mount Vernon, south of Alexandria. But did you know Washington purchased land within Arlington as well? He bought 1,000 acres of forest to use as Mount Vernon's "woodlot." It was located west of South Four Mile Run in South Arlington. In fact, if you go into the Glencarlyn Library (300 South Kensington Street), you'll find something that looks like a wooden garbage can but is actually a section of an old tree that was used as a survey marker for Washington's land. A mill built by Washington once stood along Four Mile Run, right near where the Four Mile Run Trail meets Columbia Pike.

Several historical markers commemorate a burial site where the members of the John Ball and William Carlin families were interred (Ball helped Washington survey the land and Carlin was one of Washington's tailors) and a survey marker used by George Washington in 1785.

A guided walking tour organized by the Arlington Historical Society is offered every spring.

TIP

For visitor information, contact the Arlington Historical Society.
703-892-4204
arlingtonhistoricalsociety.org

BONUS TIP
Check the historical society's website at
arlingtonhistoricalsociety.org and search for an
article by Annette that has a map and a video
that provides more details.

SOAK UP
ARLINGTON MEMORIAL BRIDGE'S SYMBOLISM

You could do a lot worse than crossing the Potomac River between Arlington and Washington, DC, on the Arlington Memorial Bridge, perhaps the most beautiful of the area's bridges. Architectural flourishes include sculptures of eagles and vases; bas-relief bison, poppies, and oak leaves; and *The Arts of War*, two massive fire-guided, bronze equestrian statues on the DC side representing Valor and Sacrifice.

But there's more. The bridge opened in 1932 to symbolically connect the North and South. Yes, we're going back to Civil War history. Robert E. Lee, the commander of the southern army, lived at Arlington House (now located inside Arlington Cemetery; see page 102), while Abraham Lincoln, president of the United States during the Civil War, is honored with the Lincoln Memorial on the river's DC side. The bridge connects the two memorials, showing the strength of a united nation after enduring such a horrific conflict.

Food for thought and opportunity for reflection as you stroll across this symbolic bridge on its wide walkway.

Over the Potomac River between Lincoln Memorial in Washington, DC, and Arlington National Cemetery in Arlington, 703-235-1530
nps.gov/gwmp/planyourvisit/memorialave.htm

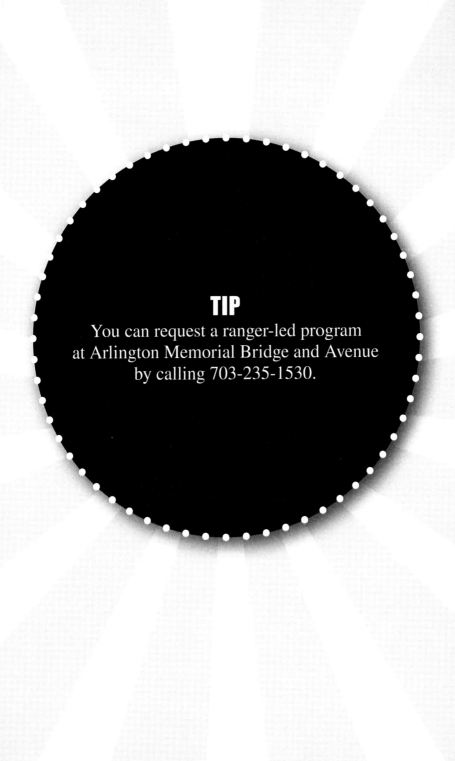

TIP
You can request a ranger-led program
at Arlington Memorial Bridge and Avenue
by calling 703-235-1530.

TRY TO FIND HISTORIC ABINGDON PLANTATION
AT DCA

If you have some extra time at Reagan Washington National Airport (DCA), seek out the ruins of a historic plantation. That's right— hidden in between the two parking garages, you'll discover a little park harboring what's left of Abingdon Plantation.

Originally built in 1695, the plantation was owned by the Alexander family (of Alexandria fame). John Parke Custis, Martha Washington's son, purchased the property in 1778 and moved his family here.

Abingdon existed as a homestead until after the Civil War when its owners fled south. The plantation deteriorated, finally burning down in 1930. When DCA was being built in the early '40s, the historical remains would have been destroyed but for the intervention of historian Eleanor Lee Templeman.

There's a little pathway circling the ruins and placards telling the story, including illustrations depicting what the original house looked like. No signs, however, mention anything about the enslaved individuals who were forced to work the land. It's an interesting juxtaposition with jumbo jets taking off in the distance.

Ronald Reagan National Airport, accessible from Terminal 2
via a walkway to Parking One
hmdb.org/m.asp?m=8381

LEND A BOOK, TAKE A BOOK
AT LITTLE FREE LIBRARIES

Looking for something good to read? Of course, we have excellent libraries from which to borrow books—Arlington's libraries are some of the best in the nation. But we also have a trove of Little Free Libraries tucked away in our neighborhoods. Scout troops and students built some as service projects, while many residents have installed their own. It's fun to take a bike ride or walk to seek out these little gems. You can find some of them using the map at littlefreelibrary.org/ourmap.

GET INSPIRED
BY ARLINGTON ARTISTS

No doubt about it, Arlington is artsy. Earlier entries have presented ways you can make your own art (and find your flow; see page 94), but you can also be inspired by the works of others. Here are some small galleries that always have something new and interesting going on. If you're motivated, maybe you'll even join in the art-making yourself!

Columbia Pike Artist Studios: Twenty-one working studio spaces for artists. They are open for special events, including the biannual open studio weekend and by appointment with individual artists.

Founders Gallery @ Mason Square: Gallery exhibitions and public programs showcase the work of grad students in an experiential learning environment.

Fred Schnider Gallery of Art: Local artists on display. Gallery Underground: Established and emerging artists are included in monthly exhibits, special exhibitions, and art workshops.

LAC Art: A mini gallery with works by resident artists.

Salon Arlington: Artists, authors, craftspeople, and musicians present their work every two months at the Village Sweet Bakery in the Westover neighborhood.

Columbia Pike Artist Studios
932 S Walter Reed Dr.
columbiapikeartiststudios.org

Founders Gallery @ Mason Square
Van Metre Hall Lobby, Mason Square Campus
3351 N Fairfax Dr.
artsmanagement.gmu.edu/about/founders-gallery

Fred Schnider Gallery of Art
888 N Quincy St., #102, 703-841-9404
fredschnidergalleryofart.com

Gallery Underground
The Shops at 2100 Crystal Dr., 571-483-0652
arlingtonartistsalliance.org

LAC Art
5722 Langston Blvd., 703-228-0560
arlingtonva.us/government/programs/arts/programs/lac

Salon Arlington
5872 Washington Blvd., dustyswb@verizon.net
salonarlington.com

LEARN THE HEARTBREAKING STORIES
BEHIND THE PENTAGON

The Pentagon is a looming presence in Arlington. You can't miss it if you're driving on Washington Boulevard or Route 110—it is, after all, the world's largest low-rise office space, all 6.5 million square feet of it. You can take a tour, where you'll learn that some 26,000 military and civilian workers, our neighbors and friends, show up every day, doing the work of the Department of Defense.

And it has tragic stories.

The Pentagon was built on an accelerated schedule over two years, between 1941 and 1943. Originally, it was slated to go into Arlington Farms, a temporary housing complex on the former grounds of the Custis-Lee family estate, bordered on five sides by roads, hence the five-sided shape. However, President Franklin D. Roosevelt felt the building would block the view of Washington from Arlington Cemetery, so he moved it to its current location, keeping the pentagon design. And in the process, the residents of Queen City, a tightly knit Black neighborhood, were displaced to make room, with little compensation. They were the descendants of Freedman's Village, established by the federal government during the Civil War as a place for freed enslaved individuals to live.

And then on September 11, 2001, terrorists crashed American Airlines Flight 77 into the Pentagon's western flank, killing 189 people. A memorial pays tribute to that horrific day (see page 100) and encourages us to never forget.

1 N Rotary Rd.
defense.gov/pentagon-tours/request-a-tour

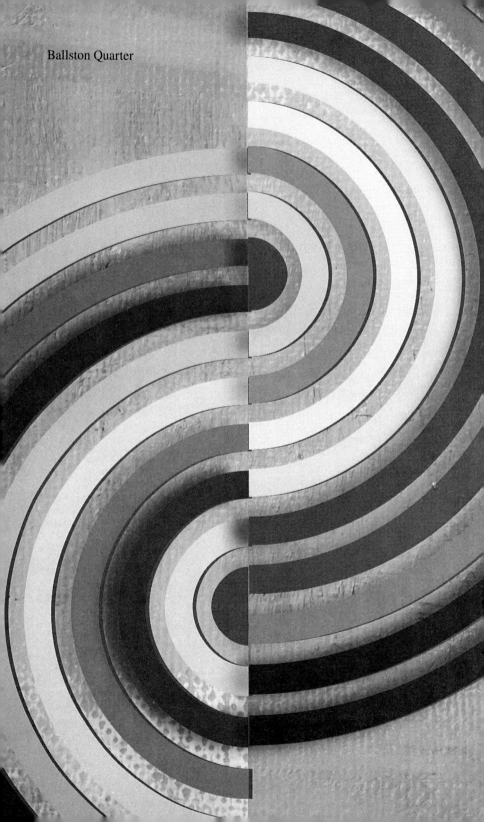

Ballston Quarter

SHOPPING
AND FASHION

FIND EVERYTHING
AT AYERS VARIETY & HARDWARE

Need a baseball bat? Mulch? Heart-shaped doilies? A tea strainer? Hair ties? Two nails? The local joke—or maybe it's more a comforting fact—is that whatever you are looking for, whatever you need, you'll find it at this one-size-fits-all variety store. John W. Ayers, a World War II vet, opened J. W. Ayers Five and Ten Cents Store in 1948. He was known as the Mayor of Westover, handing out Tootsie Pops to kids, donating materials to local classrooms, and overseeing the Westover Christmas Tree. He died in 1976, and amid concerns the store would be lost forever, the Kaplan family bought it and continues the nostalgic tradition to this day (Mr. Kaplan's daughter, Kristine Peterkin, manages the store). It's fun just to roam the aisles for serendipitous finds: placemats, seasonal decorations, house paint, flower seeds, Charleston Chews, and five things you forgot you needed. In spring and summer, high-quality plants and flowers are sold out front.

5853 Washington Blvd., Westover Village, 703-538-5678
facebook.com/profile.php?id=100063525071620

SUPPORT ARLINGTON'S OWN INDEPENDENT BOOKSTORE
AT ONE MORE PAGE BOOKS

We all love thumbing through actual books, being tempted by their covers, crisp pages, and beautiful type-printed words. Lucky Arlingtonians have the perfect place to do that—One More Page Books. That said, this independent bookshop is much more than a place to buy books. The staff is devoted to the written word, ensuring you find exactly what you need to read, whether it's from an emerging author or occupies a special niche. It's also a community hub, with fun in-store events bringing people together, including author readings (both local and national), book clubs, and wine and chocolate pairings. Eileen McGervey opened the shop in 2011, and despite recent challenges, it continues to retain its relevance. Please support this Arlington treasure!

2200 N Westmoreland St., #101, 703-300-9746
onemorepagebooks.com

SAVE THE PLANET
WHILE CLOTHES SHOPPING

One of the secrets to helping reduce waste on Earth is to recycle clothes. Instead of shopping at high-end fashion malls when you're looking for something new, head out to Arlington's consignment boutiques. You'll find several with high-quality, trendy items at reasonable prices—and you also will have a place to donate gently used clothes that are filling space in your closet.

Amalgamated Costume and Design Studio: If you're looking for vintage, this shop is well-known in the mid-Atlantic region for its range of clothing from the turn of the 20th century to the 1960s.

Blossom & Buds: This consignment shop in Westover specializes in women's and children's clothing, shoes, and accessories. You'll find famous brand names like Lululemon, Madewell, Patagonia, Kate Spade, and Anthropologie. Amber Mustafa of Fairlington opened this little jewel in 2020. You can shop this store online as well.

Current Boutique: Carmen Lopez owns three accolade-winning shops in Northern Virginia and DC, including this one in Clarendon, where you'll find racks of chic items from Badgley Mischka, Ted Baker, Tory Burch, and Kate Spade, just to name a few. There's an online component as well.

Amalgamated Costume and Design Studio
5179-B Langston Blvd., 703-517-7373
amalgamated-clothing.com

Blossom & Buds
5906 Washington Blvd., 703-241-9227
blossomandbuds.com

Current Boutique
2601 Wilson Blvd., 703-528-3079
currentboutique.com

SHOP FAIR TRADE
AT TRADE ROOTS

You will find the best combination of boutique and heart at this fair-trade, eco-friendly shop in Westover. A foray inside reveals shelves and tables filled with colorful ceramics, bags made from recycled tires, handblown wine glasses, sterling silver bracelets, dog paraphernalia, and more. Purchasing these fun products and handcrafted items made by creatives from large cities and remote villages around the world ensures each artisan is paid a living wage. On the Trade Roots website, shop owner Lisa Ostroff writes, "By purchasing fair trade products, you are taking a step toward alleviating poverty in developing communities, allowing many people to escape city slums by allowing them to work from home, and even creating avenues for literacy, banking, and clean water projects."

But that's not all. Trade Roots also offers fair-trade coffee, tea, wine, beer, and baked goods to enjoy at tables sprinkled around the front of the shop, as well as on the tree-shaded front lawn. Needless to say, it's a welcoming neighborhood place.

5852 Washington Blvd., Westover Village, 571-335-4274
fairtraderoots.com

SUPPORT LOCAL
AT TWO THE MOON

Former nurse Johanna Braden dreamed of starting a neighborhood gift shop, and that is what she did in 2014 in the Williamsburg Shopping Center. In this jam-packed boutique, you'll find all kinds of fun and whimsical goodies, including greeting cards, soy candles, coffee table books, candlesticks, painted bowls, coffee mugs, and wall art—plus a children's section of books and toys. Local companies are featured, including food items from DC's Gordy's Pickle Jar and gorgeous jewelry designed by Arlington-based Ruth Barzel. But what makes this place especially unique is its focus on local-centric items—wine glasses and cocktail napkins emblazoned with the 22207 zip code; travel mugs imprinted with JMU, VCU, Virginia Tech, and other nearby places our kids and friends might be headed off to college; Nats and Caps T-shirts; and more. Braden also offers embroidery services and vinyl monogramming on-site, to make that gift extra special.

6501 N 29th St. in Williamsburg Shopping Center, 703-300-9340
twothemoon.com

SAY OH LÀ LÀ
AT LE VILLAGE MARCHÉ

No need to jump on a plane to Paris when we have this adorable French-inspired boutique in Shirlington. With French café music floating through the air, it's fun to stroll among the perfectly appointed shelves and be tempted by lavender soaps, French-made tea towels, handmade notecards, Ladurée recipe books, La Rochelle glassware decorated with fleur-de-lys, unique jewelry, and more. There are some interesting salvaged items here, too, such as door handles and iron finials turned into wine stoppers, not to mention vintage furniture such as antique armoires. Angela Phelps opened the shop in 2005, and it's the next best thing to browsing Paris's neighborhood markets. No doubt, there's something here for tout le monde.

2800 S Randolph St., Ste. 110A, Shirlington Village, 703-379-4444
levillagemarche.com

EMBRACE YOUR INNER CHILD
AT KINDER HAUS TOYS

This 5,000-square-foot, old-fashioned wonderland of games, toys, books, clothes, and stuffed animals in Shirlington is every child's dream come true. Kids come alive as they wander the labyrinth of shelves overflowing with toys that—get this—are mostly powered by imagination, not batteries; many of the toys are made of wood. Hot products include 3D magnetic building tiles, *Star Wars* LEGO, Green Toys Dump Trucks, and Replogle Globes. The children's book corner presents classics along with the newer Caldecott Award–winning books. It's a toy store you can feel good about.

1220 N Fillmore St., Shirlington Village, 703-527-5929
kinderhaus.com

TIP

Another amazing independent toy store is Child's Play! in Lee Heights Shops, with two floors of toys, books, sporting goods—and free gift wrap.
4510 Cherry Hill Rd., 703-522-1022
childsplaytoysandbooks.com

NEVER WORRY ABOUT FINDING THE PERFECT GIFT FOR ANYONE EVER AGAIN
AT THE URBAN FARMHOUSE

Tucked into the downstairs of a historic farmhouse on Wilson Boulevard, the Urban Farmhouse is one of two gifty boutiques you'll find inside. It's beautifully decorated, exactly as an urban farmhouse should look, with shelves and country-style furniture painted in cheery colors and displaying a tempting array of items. There are gift books, notecards, magic wands, home decor, barware, cheery serving ware, fun puzzles, and spices. The framed paintings by Virginia artist Dee Dee Volinsky, by the way, are especially desirable. Some of the furniture is for sale, too. The only danger here is that you might very well find something for yourself while shopping for your friends.

5140 Wilson Blvd., 703-718-4897
theurbanfarmhousestore.com

● ●

GO CRAZY WITH ARLINGTON-CENTRIC DECOR
AT COVET

The second you enter Covet, the second boutique in the historic Wilson Boulevard farmhouse (upstairs), you'll notice the aroma. It smells so good in here! Explore a little further and you'll find all kinds of candles and essential oils to make your home smell just as nice. Oh, except you're here looking for a friend, right? There's also home decor, cocktail mixes, jewelry, local art, and children's clothes . . . though perhaps what Covet really does well is the wide selection of Arlington-imprinted items, including coasters, wall art, dish towels ("Someone in Arlington Loves Me"), glasses ("Real Housewives of Arlington"), and shopping bags sporting a whimsical map of our county-city. You can also commission a custom house or pet drawing by a local artist. Complimentary gift wrapping is offered—gift buying has never been easier.

5140B Wilson Blvd., 703-247-9797
covetinarlington.com

Columbia Marina

ACTIVITIES
BY SEASON

SPRING

SUMMER

• •

FALL

WINTER

SUGGESTED
ITINERARIES

THE MAJORS

ART AFFAIR

SPORTS LOVERS

WORK OUT

THE GREAT OUTDOORS

HISTORY BUFFS

• •

KID FRIENDLY

Enjoy a Traditional Campfire with S'mores at Long Branch Nature Center, 64

Enjoy Good, Old-Fashioned Family Fun at the Arlington County Fair, 47

Embrace Your Inner Child at Kinder Haus Toys, 131

Revel in a Celestial Show at the David M. Brown Planetarium, 46

NIGHT OUT

Relish the Best of Off-Broadway at Signature Theatre, 34

Hang Out at Northside Social, 28

Relax with a Pint and Live Music at Westover Market Beer Garden, 42

Celebrate a Special Occasion at Sfoglina, 25

DO SOME GOOD

Support Arlington's Own Independent Bookstore at One More Page Books, 125

Help the Food Insecure at a Little Food Pantry, 31

Shop Fair Trade at Trade Roots, 128

Be Socially Conscious at Busboys and Poets, 39

Save the Planet While Clothes Shopping, 126

Rip Out Invasive Plants, 61

LEARNING FOR FUN

UNDER-THE-RADAR FOODIE MECCAS

OFF THE BEATEN PATH

• •

INDEX

Air Force Memorial